Andrew Bibby is a freelance writer and journalist, and a regular contributor to *The Independent* and other newspapers and magazines. He was born in 1953, and currently lives in Coventry.

His family's links with Purbeck date back to 1918 when his grandfather, stationed in an army camp near Swanage, was taken with the beauty of the countryside around him. His family returned to Purbeck each year thereafter, and Andrew Bibby has continued this tradition, now visiting the area several times a year with his own family. He has walked all the walks included in the book, many of them more than once, and brings a fresher perspective to the Purbecks that should delight both residents and visitors alike.

Frontispiece
Clavell Tower, Kimmeridge

Walking in Purbeck

Andrew Bibby

Line drawings by Philip Winton
Maps by Louise Dobbs

THE DOVECOTE PRESS

I dedicate this book to the memory of my mother
MARJORIE SAUNDERS BIBBY
who also walked in Purbeck
and who also wrote of what she found

First published in 1989 by the Dovecote Press Ltd
Stanbridge, Wimborne, Dorset BH21 4JD

Reprinted 1992

ISBN 0 946159 64 5

Photoset in Palatino by Character Graphics, Taunton, Somerset
Printed and bound by Biddles Ltd, Guildford and King's Lynn

Contents

11. Kimmeridge – Smedmore Hill – Swyre Head – Coast Path – Kimmeridge Bay – Kimmeridge

12. Kimmeridge – Gad Cliff – Worbarrow – Tyneham – Kimmeridge Bay – Kimmeridge

13. Lulworth Cove – Flowers Barrow – Tyneham – Worbarrow – Lulworth Cove

14. Corfe Castle – Scotland Farm – Norden Heath – Blue Pool – Norden Wood – Corfe Castle

15. Arne – Shipstal Point – Arne

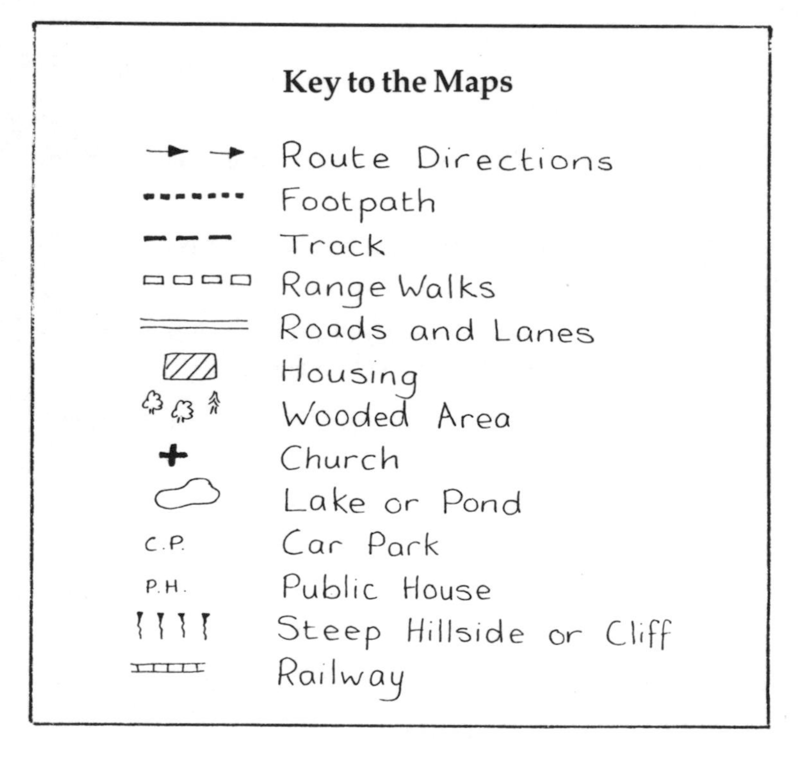

Introduction

In Purbeck, it's easy to enjoy walking. Of course, the area has many other attractions, and if you're here on holiday I wouldn't necessarily want to drag you away from the beaches at Swanage and Studland all the time. But nevertheless it would be a shame to visit Purbeck, and not see something of the countryside: and there's no doubt that the best way to do this is on foot. Fortunately, that's not difficult: there is a comprehensive network of rights of way, most of which are well-marked and well-walked.

Purbeck offers startling contrast in a relatively small geographical area – as you'll appreciate if you explore even a handful of the walks in this book. There's the long ridge of chalk hills, running coast-to-coast from Ballard Point to Worbarrow Bay. There's the coast itself, with high cliffs, little coves and, of course, fine sea views. There's the quiet valley of the Corfe river, and the limestone ridge of Swyre Head to Gad Cliff. And there's also the heathland.

Fifteen walks means that you could tackle one each day of a two-week holiday, and still have one left for another visit. But I hope you won't feel compelled to follow the walks slavishly. If the walks seem too long, or if you have young children, then have no compunction in just walking part of the way. Alternatively, if you're a keen walker and feel let down that the longest walk here is a measly eight miles, then of course tackle two or three together.

Choosing the walks has been an enjoyable process, but inevitably some good footpaths have had to be left out. I've opted for variety, and tried to include some walks which explore lesser-known parts of Purbeck. But I've also included the obvious favourites. I'd like to think that the book will be useful to visitors who don't as yet know the area very well and want to be pointed in the right direction, as well as those who know Purbeck better. I also hope that the walks will appeal both to committed ramblers and to those who just fancy a good stroll.

I decided early on that the walks should be circular, and should begin and end in towns or villages. I try to indicate what facilities are available to the tired or hungry walker in each place, and whether the routes are serviced by public transport. I also give some idea of the length of each walk and the time it will take to walk it – though treat the mileage distances with some caution. Two miles of up-and-down clifftop walking (as near Arish Mell, for example) easily equals three miles of heathland walking. The same applies to time: where one person might stride, another might stroll – or even stop for a picnic.

Although the book includes sketch-maps, I strongly suggest that you acquire one of the Ordance Survey 1:25,000 maps of the area – the Outdoor Leisure map "Purbeck" is widely available and covers all the walks in the book, but it's also worth considering the cheaper and less cumbersome Sheet SY87/97/SZ07, confusingly also called "Purbeck", which will be all you need for everything except walks (13) and (15).

The detailed instructions for each walk were correct at the time of writing, and I have of course walked each path at least once while compiling the book. But the countryside is a living place. There will be changes during the lifetime of this book, and not every waymark or landmark mentioned will necessarily remain always as it was. Nevertheless, I don't think you'll find it easy to get seriously lost while walking in Purbeck.

Look down from Ballard Down or the Corfe hill towards Poole and Bournemouth, and by contrast Purbeck seems, by some lucky chance, to have remained wonderfully unspoilt. That's not to say, however that human activity hasn't left a profound mark on the landscape as I hope this book will make clear. Both in the past and certainly today Purbeck has been the scene of considerable industrial activity – stone, marble, clay, shale and now, most dramatically of all, oil from the massive reserves underneath Purbeck, which are being tapped by BP at their Wytch Farm site. Agriculture, too, as all walkers should remember, is a business: as one Church Knowle resident graphically put it to me once, "every blade of grass has a price label on it".

But understanding that the Purbeck countryside is a place of economic activity should enhance our understanding, and the pleasures to be got from walking here, rather than detracting from the experience. I wish you very happy walking; perhaps we'll meet on the way.

Acknowledgements

Many people have helped me in the preparation of this book. I am particularly grateful to Jane Scullion and to my father Noel Bibby for their many useful comments and suggestions.

I also acknowledge the assistance given, shortly before her death, by Mary Baxter of the Ramblers Association in Purbeck.

1. Swanage – Old Harry Rocks – Studland – Ballard Down – Swanage

A classic walk of about four miles taking 1½ – 2½ hours from Swanage beach past the Old Harry Rocks to Studland village, and back across Ballard Down.

Starting point Swanage beach (New Swanage end). Park in the North Beach car park (at the end of De Moulham Road), or in neighbouring roads. It's sometimes possible to find places to park in or near Burlington Road (off Ulwell Road), in which case a footpath leads directly to the beach.

Buses run along the front between Swanage and Studland and Bournemouth; and to Swanage town from Corfe Castle, Wareham and Poole.

Facilities Studland has a pleasant pub, the Bankes Arms; there are also a number of shops, a beach cafe, and several hotels providing meals. Toilets.

Problems None, although take appropriate care at the cliff edge.

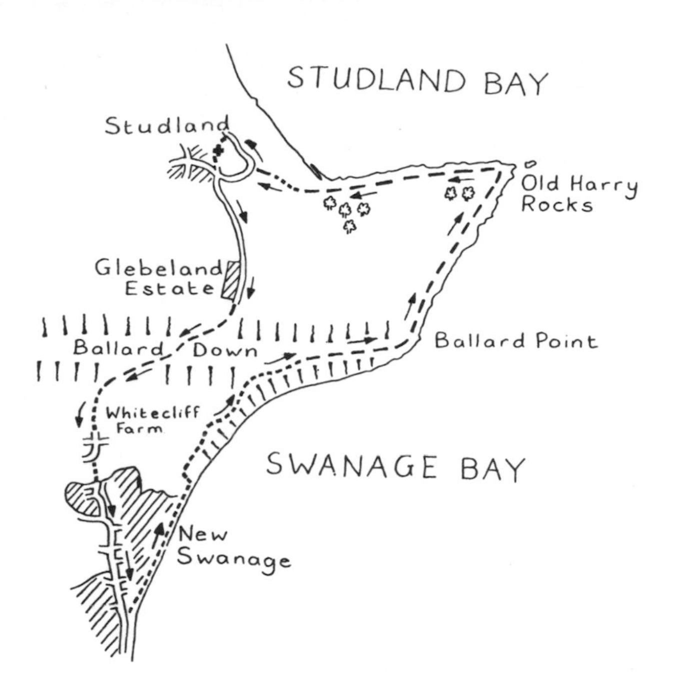

DESCRIPTION

The Old Harry Rocks used to feature as one of the framed illustrations on the walls of railway compartments, in the days when railway carriages had such things. Nowadays, the pictures have gone and British Rail is no longer able to bring you straight to Swanage – but Old Harry remains a famous Purbeck landmark, rivalling Corfe Castle for a place on the picture postcards and on the cover of travel brochures.

I'm tempted to say that, if you think you only have the time or inclination to do one walk, this should be the one – because I suspect that having walked around Ballard Point and down to Old Harry you'll change your mind. Studland is a fine destination for a walk, too – the wonderful sandy beach, a well-situated village pub, and the superb unspoilt Norman church should cater for most tastes. (I recommend all three).

The Old Harry Rocks pair up with the similar chalk stacks at the Needles, on the Isle of Wight, which are often clearly visible from Swanage. In times past, the chalk downs used to continue unbroken across what is now the English Channel, and Poole Harbour and the Solent were simply a river valley. The sea, having very successfully separated Wight from the mainland still nibbles away at Old Harry. One of the stacks, which had been named Old Harry's Wife, was washed away in a storm in 1896; in exchange, the sea periodically separates new stacks from the main body of chalk, so that Old Harry's family stays much the same size from generation to generation.

The Pinnacles and Old Harry Rocks

The path around Old Harry is one of the most popular in Purbeck, and you won't need to worry about getting lost. The cliffs deserve respect, however, and can be dangerous to anyone foolhardy enough to leave the path, as the records in Swanage lifeboat station demonstrate. Reckless holidaymakers are not a new phenomenon; C. E. Robinson in his book *Picturesque Rambles in the Isle of Purbeck* published in 1882 has a story dating from a few years earlier: 'It occurred to a pair of Londoners, on a visit to Swanage, to try the excitement of a little home alpine climbing. Soon enough they reached the point from which ascent or descent was equally difficult. Dusk rapidly came on, and during the whole night – one of rain and wind – there they stood, hungry and cold, with their backs to the inhospitable rock. A dense mist hid them from view the next morning, but, though not seen, their cries were heard on board the steamer from Poole, and a party of coastguardsmen were sent out in search. But it was late in the afternoon before the two crestfallen victims of this unlucky adventure were rescued, by means of ropes let down from the top.'

But who needs this sort of extra excitement, when the walk itself has so many pleasures to offer?

DIRECTIONS

Walk along Swanage sea-front away from the town along the promenade. When the sea-wall and huts finally stop, keep on the beach past three breakwaters. Just before the fourth and final breakwater, turn left up a row of steps, and then almost immediately right up some more steps.

You are now on the coast path, which climbs slowly, skirting the cliff-edge. There are fine views to be had back over Swanage beach and bay. The path marks the geological transition to the chalk hills by climbing more steeply, and the fields to the left give way to open downland. Continue straight ahead (ignore two stiles on the left) until you reach a series of earthworks (a triangulation stone, a concrete pillar used for map-making, lies a little way over to the left). Carry on along the side of Ballard Cliff, but take an opportunity soon to move over to join the main ridgeway path running parallel, a few yards away to the left.

The path drops quite steeply until Ballard Point is turned, and the first of the chalk stacks come into sight. Directly ahead now are the buildings of Bournemouth, across the water of Poole Bay. This is the place too to notice just how close to the edge the path ahead goes. Follow the path as it slowly loses height, until finally the last chalk stacks, the Old Harry Rocks themselves, are reached.

The chalk stacks are a refuge for the sea-birds, safe from human interference. The name on the map, St Lucas Leap, commemorates not some miraculous feat of long-jumping by an early Christian saint, but (so the story goes) an unsuccessful jump by a pedigree greyhound called St. Lucas which had belonged to a Studland squire, and which had been trying to catch a hare at the time. Alas, the dog was killed; let's hope the hare survived.

The path turns the corner, and shortly afterwards enters a little woodland. Studland and its beach lie ahead. After a few hundred yards of dusty walking, on the outskirts of Studland, continue half-right along a little footpath (a farm-track carries on half-left through fields). The path runs beside some tall evergreens, before turning into a sunken lane to emerge in Studland village beside some toilets. Turn right on to the tarmac road, and pass the Bankes Arms and the National Trust car-park.

If you want to spend time in Studland, or reach the beach, carry on along the road at this point. But to continue the walk, turn left through a gate immediately after the small N.T. car-park, into a little meadow; the churchyard is directly ahead. Enter the church-yard, and turn left once the edge of the church is reached, finally leaving along the tarmac approach road until the village cross is reached.

A detail from the Corbel table, Studland Church

Studland church is a wonderful unspoilt Norman Church, which Nikolaus Pevsner has described as one of the dozen or so most complete examples in the country. It seems likely that it was originally built before the Conquest, but rebuilt soon afterwards. Incidentally, look out for the carved stone faces – both animal and human – on the external north wall of the nave. Don't miss the gravestone of Waterloo veteran Sergeant William Lawrence to the south-west of the path.

For many years, all that was left of Studland's village cross was a stone stump. The cross you see today may look traditional – but a closer look will reveal some very twentieth century images, including Concorde. The stone came from a quarry at St Aldhelm's Head and was carved by a local marble-worker Treleven Haysom; the cross itself was erected in 1976.

At the cross keep straight ahead, taking the track beside some farm buildings. The track rapidly becomes tarmac again, and runs ahead up to the Glebeland Estate of villas on the side of the hill. Follow the road, passing a number of houses to your right, until the road finally peters out. Carry on through a gate, joining an old track which runs diagonally up the side of the hill. The path crosses a meadow before reaching the brow.

Here there is an old much-weathered stone which invites you to 'Rest and Be Thankful'. The stone was erected here in 1852 by David Jardine (his initials can be seen at the side of the stone), a Londoner who also donated a clock to Swanage parish church.

Cross the ridgeway path and continue downhill, the path falling diagonally to the right. Swanage and its bay is now in view again; directly below is Whitecliff farm. When the path reaches the limits of open downland, carry on through a little gate into a pleasant sunken track between two fields. Keep straight ahead at Whitecliff, crossing over the farm approach road.

Whitecliff farmhouse dates back to the early seventeenth century, though the site itself is mentioned in the Domesday Book. 'No more charming site for a house than that of Whitecliff can be found along the sea-coast for many a long mile', wrote C. E. Robinson in 1882. 'Such an aspect – warm, sunny, and sheltered! such beautiful views around! such fine old elms and poplars!'

Cross a stile, and take a narrow path, running between two fields, until finally a tarmac suburban road is reached. Carry on down Hill Road, turn left, and then follow the road down to the New Swanage shops. Here the main road from Studland joins from the right; follow it, initially half-left, back down to the beach.

The 'Rest and be Thankful' Seat

2. Studland – Ulwell – Ballard Down – Old Harry Rocks – Studland

A four mile walk taking 1½ – 2½ hours, initially across the heathland and then following the ridgeway path along Ballard Down, returning to Studland past the Old Harry Rocks. Arguably, one of the best walks in southern England.

Starting point Studland village. Buses from Swanage and from Bournemouth, over the toll ferry. Use the National Trust North Beach Car Park, or the smaller car park next to the Bankes Arms.

Facilities In Studland: Bankes Arms pub, shops, beach cafe, hotel meals and teas; toilets (Studland offers a wonderful sandy beach, and the village itself is worth exploring: see the introduction to Walk 1).

Problems Relatively straightforward on the heathland; very straightforward once Ballard Down is reached.

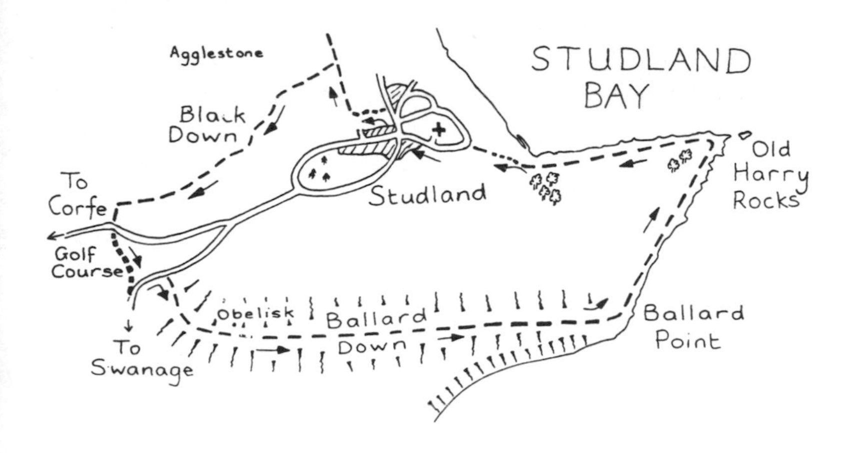

DESCRIPTION

This walk offers both heath and hills, a wonderful combination. Ballard Down is a particular favourite of mine – and I'm sure with many other thousands of walkers who have come this way.

I've walked along the springy turf on the ridgeway on fiercely hot days when the heat haze has danced off the land just ahead of the path, and when the sailing boats in Studland Bay below have been little white dots on a sea of bright blue. I can't guarantee this weather, of course: in fact, I've also stood beside the Ulwell obelisk, completely drenched, as the rain whipped in from across Godlingston Hill.

I hope you get the sunshine; but even if the weather is bad, there's something to be said for getting out the waterproofs and coming this way.

I make absolutely no apologies for including again the section of cliff walking around Ballard Point and Old Harry Rocks – if you've done Walk 1 you'll have been this way already, but I'm sure you won't mind repeating the experience. Personally, I return to do this walk again and again.

DIRECTIONS

The walk starts from the cross-roads on the main road in the centre of Studland village, by the village hall. Walk a short distance north along the main road towards the ferry, passing through a little wooded area. Just before the Studholme Hotel, turn left up a track. Keep to the right of some stables, following the path through a small wood. Cross a stile, and then cut diagonally across a small field, to another stile.

Beyond the stile, turn right along a well-worn sandy lane. The lane skirts an open pasture, before the gorse and bracken close in. Pass through a gate, and immediately turn sharp left, leaving the lane to climb up a narrow path on to the heathland.

The path is well used, not least by horse riders from the Studland stables. Keep straight ahead, ignoring various side-turnings, climbing steadily. The outlying houses in Studland village lie a little way off to the left.

The path swings round sharply to the left, shortly after another path has joined from the left. Almost immediately it bends back to the right, to run alongside a boundary wire fence. Carry on, skirting the heather-covered Black Down to your right. To your left, the obelisk at Ulwell, which the walk reaches in due course, is easy to spot.

As the golf course is approached, it's worth turning back to admire the view over the harbour. The Agglestone rock (visited in Walk 3) can also be seen, high on its mound in the middle of the heath.

Carry on until you reach a golf fairway, beside you on the right. Immediately past the green, turn sharp left, taking a narrow path between trees and bushes.

Cross the Studland-Corfe road, and climb the stile immediately opposite. You are now on the 9-hole golf course. Walk across the fairways aiming for the tallest of the trees opposite; you will find the path disappearing down the hill, through some undergrowth. A stile

The Ulwell Obelisk, Ballard Down

takes you into a large pasture; head right, to a stile on to the Swanage road.

Walk left along the main road for a hundred yards, turning first right up a track, which climbs up the side of the hills. A National Trust sign confirms the route. The main gate is likely to be carefully padlocked; only Coastguard landrovers are permitted on the ridgeway path, for cliff rescue duties. Carry on up the track to the Obelisk.

The obelisk began life in the city of London, in front of the church of St Mary Woolnoth. Like many other pieces of redundant London masonry it was carefully brought down to Swanage by George Burt, and erected on top of a bronze age barrow at Ulwell to celebrate the construction of Swanage's Ulwell waterworks. This was Burt's second attempt to improve his home town's water supply – in 1864 he had obtained an Act of Parliament to raise water from an artesian well, and had built the waterworks at the back of Sentry Road, Swanage. The obelisk was taken down in 1941, as it was considered to be too obvious a land mark for enemy planes. Most of the stone sections were reassembled by an Army working party in 1973.

You will need no detailed instructions for the next mile; the ridgeway path continues along the brow of Ballard Down, with wonderful views on both sides of the hill. Ballard Down was acquired by the National Trust, as part of their Enterprise Neptune, and the N.T. have restored the downland turf: the hilltop above Whitecliff had for a time been given over to arable farming.

Carry on along the track, until Ballard Point and the Old Harry Rocks are reached. You are retracing the route followed by Walk 1. Follow the cliff path around towards Studland.

Once the tarmac road at Studland is reached, turn left, and follow the road back to the starting point for the walk.

3. Studland – Agglestone – Godlingston Heath – Rempstone Forest – Studland

A five mile walk of 2 – 3½ hours from Studland across the heathland, visiting the Agglestone and the forestry plantations.

Starting point On the road from Studland to the Ferry, just north of Studland village. Park in the village, or the National Trust Knoll beach car park. Buses (Swanage-Studland-Sandbanks) pass.

Facilities In Studland: Bankes Arms pub, shops, beach cafe, hotel meals and teas; toilets.

Problems Can be muddy in a number of places, especially in wet weather. Generally well marked; poorly marked at Greenland.

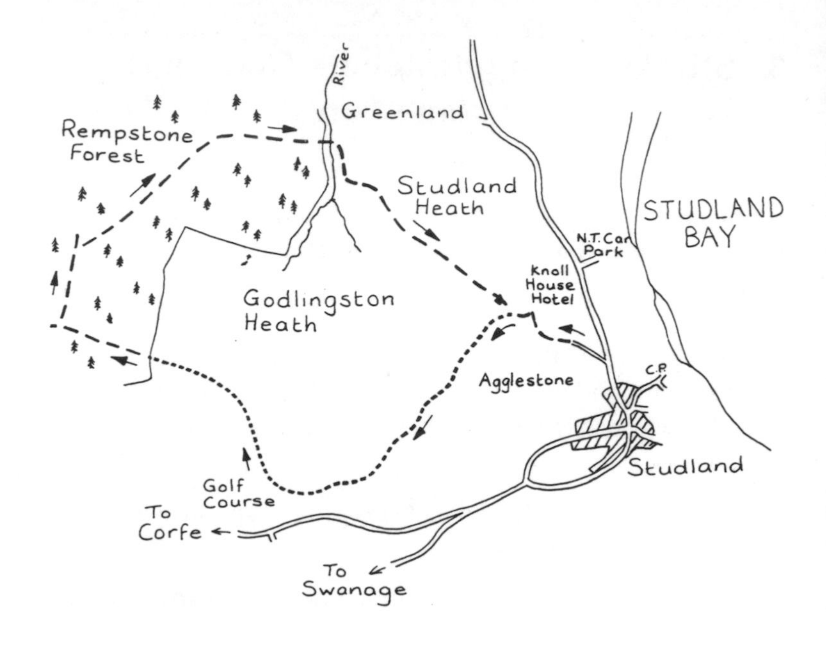

DESCRIPTION

This walk takes you into the secret part of the Isle of Purbeck, the area of wild heathland and forest which so many Swanage holidaymakers don't discover. They are missing out, for as this walk demonstrates, the heath has its own considerable beauty. You won't meet any other people whilst walking, but you will find some unspoilt countryside and some fine views. And the Agglestone, reached after only about half a mile, should be on every visitor's itinerary.

The heathland stretches across the northern half of the Isle of Purbeck, bounded by the hidden reaches of Poole Harbour in the north and the hills in the south. In fact, the heath continues beyond Purbeck, becoming the great Dorset heath which Thomas Hardy called Egdon Heath. Hardy used the setting of the heath as atmosphere for some of his novels, and in places it can seem a brooding place. In eastern Purbeck, much of the heathland was afforested after the Second World War: a mile or two of this walk is through forest paths. The walk starts and finishes, however, on Studland Heath, which has remained untouched and is now a nature reserve.

The heathland is of considerable interest to naturalists. Many rare plants can be found, including Marsh Gentian,Bog Orchid, and the conspicuously large heather called Dorset Heath, which is mainly confined to the Purbeck area. The forests are the homes for several types of deer, while all six British reptiles are to be found on the heathland, including the rare sand lizard and the smooth snake. The adder lives here too – which shouldn't discourage you, though avoid walking through undergrowth in beach sandals!

The best time to catch sight of the deer is twilight – but having said that, last time I followed this walk it was the hottest time of a hot May day, and as I approached Greenland two little roe deer watched me closely from the shelter of some trees, about twenty feet away. A little earlier, a solitary fox had emerged on to the path ahead of me, looked me up and down, and sauntered off again – so, even if humans are missing, you may share your walk with others.

DIRECTIONS

Turn left off the main road from Studland to the ferry just north of Studland village, and just past the 30 mph sign, before Studland Bay House and Knoll House Hotel are reached. Some white-painted horizontal slatted fencing marks the start of what is initially a dusty unmade road.

Carry on up the road until Wadmore farm and cottages are reached. Once past the buildings, the road becomes a track through woodland, with a wooden bridge over a stream. At the edge of the wood, a board announces the start of the Nature Conservancy Council reserve, and the Agglestone, a large rock perched on a hillock, comes into sight on your left. Turn left off the main path almost immediately, heading off across the heath until you reach the Agglestone.

The Agglestone makes a powerful impression as it rises up and above the deserted heathland. It's quite easy to understand how stories grew up locally that it was the work of the devil, whose hand slipped when throwing it from the Isle of Wight intending to demolish Salisbury Cathedral (some say Corfe Castle). In fact, the Agglestone's origins are more prosaic, but nevertheless remarkable: it is a natural phenomenon, of hard ironstone, and about 500 tons, which has remained in place while the surrounding heath has been eroded over the millenia. Part of the Agglestone's effect comes from its setting. Its name, Agglestone, may mean 'holy stone', or it may mean 'witch stone'.

Carry on past the Agglestone (turn round for some fine views over Poole Harbour). After a few hundred yards, the edge of the Purbeck golf course is reached. At the first way-mark stone, follow the sign to Studland road. A series of markers take you along the edge of some fairways; continue until you find a sign directing you off right towards Rempstone Forest. Take this, and when the path splits almost immediately turn left, again following a sign to Rempstone.

For the next half-mile the path meanders along the edge of the golf course, from one stone marker to another. As you reach the furthest edges of the golf course, the path again splits, and again you follow the left turn. (The right hand turn, signed to 'Greenland the forest', is a short-cut, saving about half a mile, but missing most of the forest walk).

Once away from the golf course, you are quickly at the edge of the forest. Carry straight along a forest track, until after about 300 yards you reach a T-junction. Turn right, and again carry on for some hundred yards along a pleasant forestry track.

The Agglestone

Don't miss your next right turn, up a grassy path away from the more defined track you have been walking along. It's the first main opening in the forest on your right hand side; an indistinct blue waymark on a tree confirms that this is the place to turn. You are now in the heart of Rempstone Forest, amongst densely planted conifers. At a five-way junction of paths, beside a fire look-out platform, keep straight ahead (again, the track you follow is less well defined than the other tracks).

After a third of a mile, the forest thins out a little, and the path becomes a forest road. Keep straight ahead, until finally you reach the edge of the forest.

Turn left, and go through a small wooden gate (blue waymark) into a wood, and immediately across some stepping stones across a stream. You emerge from the wood at Greenland.

Greenland Farm is well named: the green fields contrast

Rempstone Stone Circle

with the heather and gorse covered heathland, from which they were created. Greenland is almost on the edge of Poole Harbour, which is just north of here, sadly out of sight. Also nearby is Newton, named from an abortive attempt in 1286 by Edward I to create a new town on this site, as a rival to powerful Poole across the water. More recently, this area was the scene of a large-scale clay mining operation: a narrow-gauge railway ran to Goathorn Peninsular, where boats were located with ball clay to be shipped to the Potteries.

It's hard to picture this industrial activity today; but appearances are deceptive. Beneath the heath, and underneath Poole

Bay as well, is the massive Wytch Farm oil field. This is the largest on-shore oil field in Europe, and BP have recently discovered that the reserves are even greater than they anticipated.

An initial oil well sunk at Wytch Farm, a mile or two away on the edge of Poole Harbour, has been joined in recent years by other wells, including one set deep in the woodland of Goathorn, close to Greenland. BP are well aware that their operations have to take place in a particularly beautiful and environmentally sensitive area. Comprehensive surveys of the heathland – even to the extent of commissioning maps detailing the location of every Dorset Heath plant – have been undertaken. Exercises regularly take place to test the ability of the authorities to deal with an oil spill in Poole Harbour. However, there is no doubt that the oil industry provides a very real challenge – some would say threat – to Purbeck's status as an area of outstanding natural beauty.

Greenland is the only really tricky part of this walk – and your Ordnance Survey map won't help that much. On leaving the little wood, turn right beyond a small shed, joining a farm track. Carry on through a metal gate, and into a field. Keep along the right hand side of this field, through another gate, and then turn immediately left. Walk up this field, keeping initially close to the left-hand fence, but aiming for the gate in the middle of the far fence.

Once through the gate, continue almost straight ahead: the path disappears between some gorse bushes, and emerges in a patch of open ground. Turn half right, and follow a track down a slight rise. Almost immediately you should reach a wooden gate in a wire fence, around which is a very wet and boggy patch of ground. You need to get through this bog, and the gate; once beyond, the path is well-defined and easy, running back across Studland Heath to the point where you turned off initially to go to the Agglestone. Return past Wadmore cottages to the Studland road.

4. Ulwell – Nine Barrow Down – Corfe Castle – Little Woolgarston – Ulwell

Four miles along the ridge of the Purbeck Hills to Corfe Castle, and four miles back, taking anything from 3 – 5½ hours. If eight miles seems too far, the walk can be turned into a one-way trip, with public transport used to get you back from Corfe.

Starting point Ulwell, in the gap between the hills on the Swanage-Studland road. Park in the lay-by, beside the waterworks at Ulwell (there are two lay-bys: choose the one further from Swanage). The Swanage-Studland bus passes, and there is a bus stop at the start of the walk.

Facilities Corfe Castle is a convenient half-way point to the walk: there are shops, four pubs, cafes (including National Trust tea-rooms overlooking the castle); public toilets. Buses from Wareham and Swanage.

Problems The outward walk is one of the most popular in Purbeck, and should provide no difficulties. One short stretch of path on the return leg, near Little Woolgarston, may be a little overgrown.

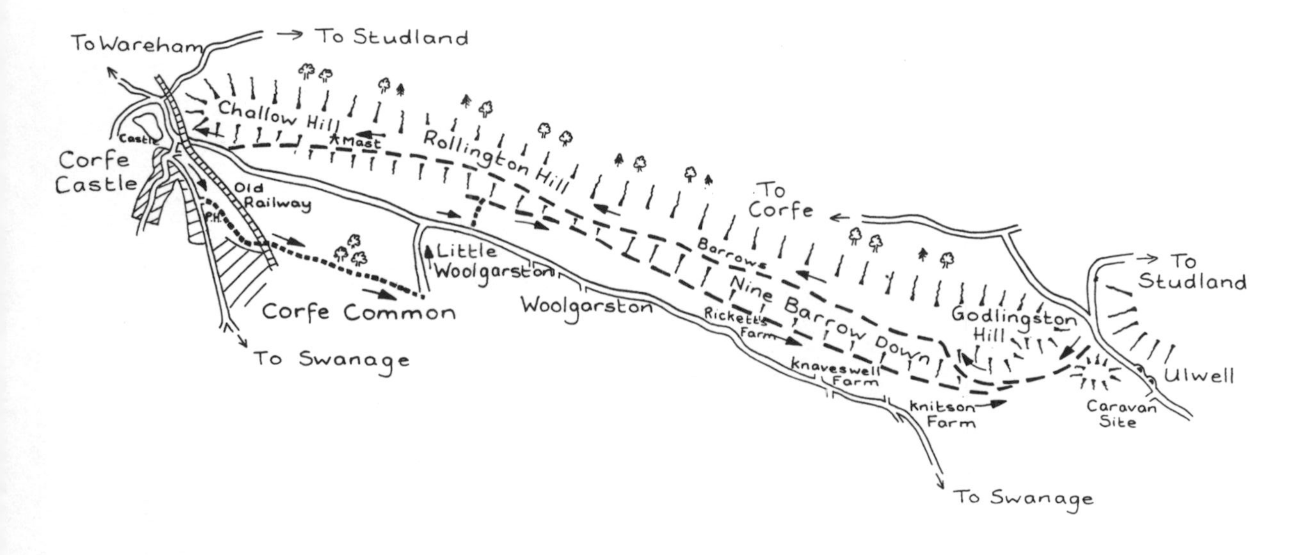
To Wareham
To Studland
Castle
Corfe Castle
Challow Hill
Mast
Rollington Hill
Old Railway
P.H.
To Corfe
Little Woolgarston
Barrows
Nine Barrow Down
Corfe Common
Woolgarston
Ricketts Farm
Godlingston Hill
To Studland
To Swanage
Knaveswell Farm
Knitson Farm
Ulwell
Caravan Site
To Swanage

DESCRIPTION

"If one wanted to show a foreigner England, perhaps the wisest course would be to take him to the final section of the Purbeck Hills, and stand him on their summit, a few miles to the east of Corfe", asserted E. M. Forster in his novel *Howard's End*. Forster duly arranged for one of his characters, Frieda Liesecke, to be escorted here, to gaze down over the Dorset heathland, the waters of Poole Harbour, and the distant hills beyond.

The 'walk to Corfe' is a popular one, and not just in fiction. The delight is not just in sharing with the sheep the ridgeway path along the longest unbroken section of the Purbeck Hills. It is also in having the village of Corfe Castle as the target for the walk. Every guide book will tell you that this is one of the most unspoilt villages in the country, but somehow Corfe always seems more attractive and even more worth visiting if you have just walked four miles to get there.

The path along the hill-top seems to slop gradually down towards Corfe, so that once you have successfully completed the first slow climb from Ulwell the walk becomes a pleasant easy stroll. Over to the left the villages of Langton and Kingston are in view, with the English Channel beyond, while Corfe village – and finally the castle itself – gradually come into sight ahead of you. On the other side of the ridgeway is the view over the heathland and harbour which Forster's characters came to see – though you'll have to walk a few yards off the path, to reach the brow of the hill, to get the full effect.

My route back from Corfe is less frequently walked and less spectacular, but with its own delights. The best moment perhaps is when you clamber up a little hillock at the edge of Corfe Common, and suddenly see the cottages at Little Woolgarston lying below you. One of them dates back to the eighteenth century: a combination of Purbeck stone and thatch and set in a wonderful garden, it is the sort of place which fuels a thousand retirement fantasies.

The final section, along the side of the Purbeck hills, will normally be shared just with the rabbits and the birds. Last time I walked it a pair of yellowhammers flitted ahead of me, the yellow of their heads matching perfectly the yellow gorse on which they were alighting.

DIRECTIONS

The walk begins at a metal gate just south of the fork in the Swanage-Studland road, where the back road from Corfe joins it. When coming from Swanage, pass Ulwell Cottage, the two lay-bys, and the entrance to the waterworks, ignoring the little stile you pass on your left.

At the time of writing, the gate has a firm 'No Parking' sign attached to it, though no waymark. Follow the chalky track upwards, passing the side of Round Down on your left. The track climbs slowly, curving round to the right, before finally reaching the brow of the hill.

Turn left at the brow, and follow the well-worn path across a number of fields. Passing through a gate, the path continues beside a wire fence, until it emerges just to the left of a cluster of barrows.

Nine Barrow Down, looking towards Ballard Down

Despite the name 'Nine Barrow Down' archaeologists have detected 17 round barrows, dating back to the Bronze Age (probably some time between 1700 BC and 1000 BC), as well as one long barrow over 110 feet long, which goes back earlier still, to the neolithic period which began around 3500 BC.

This part of Purbeck is rich in prehistoric remains: just at the foot of the hill, slightly north-west from here, are the remains of the Rempstone stone circle, now lost in an overgrown wood. The circle probably dates back to the early Bronze Age, about four thousand years ago.

Shortly beyond the barrows, you should get your first glimpse of the ruins of Corfe Castle. Initially, all there will be to see is a rough triangle of stone, emerging as if from the side of the hill in the distance ahead. Only gradually does this expand and broaden, until at last the whole castle, set on its mound in a gap in the hills, emerges fully into sight.

The path continues, leaving National Trust land, and becomes a well-defined farm-track. When this track bends sharply to the left, carry straight on. From here on, the path slopes gently down. At a telecommunications mast, you finally leave the brow of the hill, the path descending diagonally down the hillside, to emerge after a few hundred yards at a by-road. Turn right, and walk along the road for a short distance. After the old railway bridge, turn left at the main road, to reach the centre of Corfe village.

Corfe can be enjoyed without any kind of guide book – though if you want to know its full history, that is what you will need. The castle, now National Trust, is perhaps more impressive as a ruin than it ever could have been before its destruction by the Parliamentary forces during the Civil War. It stands on a natural mound, in a gap in the Purbeck Hills.

Not surprisingly, Corfe was for many centuries the most important town in Purbeck, sending members to Parliament.

If you want to visualise the castle and village as they were at the time of the Civil War, the model village offers a scaled-down reconstruction. The little museum, underneath the old Town Hall, is packed with local relics, from dinosaur footprints to signs from the Swanage branch railway.

Corfe village is essentially two roads, East Street (the main road) and West Street, which leads only out to Corfe Common.

Corfe Castle

West Street in particular is worth exploring, with many delightful Purbeck stone cottages. Despite its popularity, the village is remarkably unspoilt, with a relatively modest number of gift shops. The view from the garden of the National Trust tea-rooms must be one of the best in Britain.

Walk a short distance along East Street (the main road towards Swanage), passing on your left the seventeenth century Mortons House Hotel, a small cemetery, and a school. Immediately past the school, before you reach the Castle Inn, turn left. After a few yards, turn right across a school playing field, and then diagonally across the field beyond, aiming for the far corner beyond a little building. Once over the stile, turn left into a lane, cross a small stream, and then follow the path round to the right. You are now walking alongside the old Corfe-Swanage railway, and the path soon drops, to enable you to cross under the railway through a small bridge.

Beyond the railway, a series of wooden supports take you across marshy ground, and the path is easily found, running alongside an old hedge, at the corner of Corfe Common. (If and when Corfe Castle finally gets a by-pass, it is likely to cross the path somewhere here). Remain alongside the hedge for about half a mile. Finally, at the brow of a hill you will find yourself looking down on the cottages at Little Woolgarston.

Little Woolgarston is one of a number of settlements along the base of the Purbeck hills, strung out along the unclassified road which saunters between deep hedges from farmhouse to farmhouse.

Cross the field in front of the houses. At the cottages, turn left up the track, past some more houses. When you reach the unclassified road turn right, for a short stretch of road walking. After a little climb, turn left off the road, taking a waymarked path which runs up towards the hills.

As you emerge on to the hills, turn right, finding the path at the base of the hill which runs the full length of the ridgeway path. (It's also possible after a few hundred yards to strike up a farm track to the brow, and return on the ridgeway path you took on the way out).

The lower path carries on, past gorse and brambles. At Knitson, another ancient settlement, the path skirts a small quarry. Almost immediately on your right you will be able to see a number of mediaeval strip lynchets (field terracing). Keep along the base of the hill, and in due course you will emerge half-way up the hill you first climbed at the start of the walk. Another few hundred yards sees you back at the road to Swanage.

5. Swanage – Durston/Tilly Whim – Anvil Point – Quarries – Swanage

This is a four mile circular walk of 1½ – 2½ hours, from the centre of Swanage to the Durlston Country Park (Globe/Tilly Whim), and back again through the old stone quarrying area.

Starting point Swanage town, by the pier. (Occasional buses run to Durlston from Swanage, in case you want to break this walk half-way).

Facilities Durlston offers a bar/restaurant and snack bar; toilets. Nearby is the Durlston Country Park information centre.

Problems Very few. The path to Durlston is popular and easy to follow. Near the lighthouse the route followed may be a little overgrown; the path back through the quarries is less busy but very straightfoward.

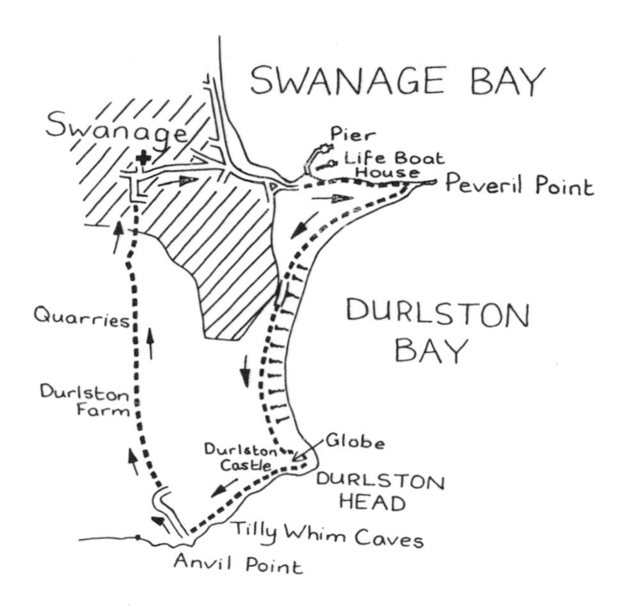

DESCRIPTION

What sort of place should Swanage be? This was the question, and the challenge, facing the town in the 1880s as the trade in Purbeck stone on which the town had (literally) been built began to fall off – and as amenities for the 'trippers' arriving in paddle-steamers from newly-developed Bournemouth began to seem more important than the massive stores of stone (the 'bankers') piled high along the foreshore.

It was also the question the town had to face almost exactly a hundred years later, in the late 1980s. A development company had acquired the site of Swanage's erstwhile grandest hotel, the Grosvenor, and wanted to build a large marina and apartment flats near the pier. But was the marina development the right way forward? The issue split the town in half: a parish poll came out against it, but the local council continued to support the plans. However, due to a legal quirk, a private bill had to be shepherded through Parliament before the marina could go ahead; late one evening in December 1987, a handful of peers turned up to vote, and by 55 votes to 45 effectively killed the scheme. (The apartments could be built without Parliamentary approval – and were). Such is the casual way that a town's history is developed.

This walk provides a chance to assess both 1880s and 1980s ideas. The walk begins at Swanage pier, beside the new apartment blocks. Once past Peveril Point, however, the late twentieth century is left behind, and we return to Victorian times, as Durlston comes into view. Durlston Country Park, now administered by the County Council, was originally the private estate of George Burt, a Swanage man who made his fortune in London, as a partner in his uncle's stone and building business. His uncle, another Swanage man, was John Mowlem, founder of the famous construction company.

George Burt returned to Swanage, determined to improve it. He laid out his Durlston estate with wide avenues and promenades, seats suitably positioned for admiring the vistas, and stone signs, appropriately inscribed with exhortations to the visitor ("Look round and read Great Nature's open Book"). There is, it seems to me, a direct link between Burt's educational plaques, which can be seen on the side of Durlston Castle and which will inform you, among other things, of the duration of the longest day at Spitsbergen, the convexity of the oceans, and the height of spring tides at Swanage, with the notices erected by the County Council around the Country Park area, and which achieve a similar tone by relaying information about Durlston's flora and fauna.

If Burt's creation of Durlston epitomises the late Victorian transformation of Swanage into a town for tourism, there are however, plenty of reminders during this walk of an earlier

Swanage. At the very start, for example, beside the Peveril flats and the 'new' pier (erected in 1896, for the pleasure boats), are the remains of the timbers of Swanage's first pier, built in 1859 purely with work in mind. Sailing boats used to tie up alongside it, ready to ship Purbeck stone to London (where it was used extensively for paving the streets) and elsewhere. A tramway was also built, from the stone stacks or bankers to the pier (remains of the tracks can still be seen set in the pavement), the stone being taken out to the pier on horse-drawn wagons. Before the pier was constructed – and even afterwards, too – horses had to draw carts loaded with stone into the shallow waters of the bay; small boats then conveyed the stone further out to sea, where ships would be riding at anchor, waiting to receive their cargo.

The stone itself came from the quarries and mines of Swanage, Herston and Langton (92 were functioning in 1878), which had been operated for generations by Purbeck's tight-knit quarrying families. The walk back from Durlston passes through some of the old quarrying areas near Townsend, Swanage.

DIRECTIONS

Walk down the Swanage High Street, towards the pier. Pass the entrance to the pier itself (and ignore the small track just beyond to Marine Villas and the Sailing Club), but then turn left just before the new Peveril development. Follow the path beside the foreshore until the last house on the right is past. On your right are some stone steps in the side of the cliff wall: climb up, and you will find yourself beside the lookout station at Peveril Point.

Peveril is still one of the most pleasant parts of Swanage, and the centre of the small lobster fishing industry.

As you walk along the foreshore near the sailing club, there's a chance to admire the 'clock tower', a typical piece of Victorian gothic architecture which was originally erected near London Bridge to commemorate the Duke of Wellington. Unfortunately for the good Duke, his tower was soon found to hold back the London traffic – whereupon John Mowlem's firm dismantled it, and shipped it to Swanage. The clock tower (incidentally, the clock itself never arrived at Swanage) is one of a number of relics from London, which Mowlem and Burt were responsible for bringing here – their motives must have been partly pragmatic, since the masonry helped provide ballast for the otherwise empty stone boats on the return journeys.

The lifeboat station has been a landmark in this part of Swanage since 1875, when a south-east gale and a dark night conspired to drive an Exeter ship, the *Wild Wave*, on to the rocks at Peveril. Fortunately, the crew of five were saved by coastguards, but it was clear that they were lucky. The town needed a lifeboat, and got one almost immediately: the story of the rescue appeared in *The Times*, and the next day one of the readers came forward with money for the boat.

The Swanage lifeboat-house is occasionally open to visitors, and the boat itself is a fine sight, particularly when being launched down the slipway into the bay. It is frequently needed to assist holidaymakers in trouble, but the Purbeck coastline remains treacherous for commercial shipping, too. The Peveril Ledges, for example, which stretch out seawards from Peveril Point, need to be given a wide berth.

Keep the coastguard look-out on your left, and follow the rough path uphill along the edge of the cliff. Swanage's second bay, Durlston Bay, is now below you; Durlston Castle, a Victorian Gothic fake, can be seen ahead at the end of the bay.

The path continues along the cliff-side before leaving the grassy hillside by a stone seat. When you reach a tarmac road, turn left (an old stone sign confirms the way), and after only about forty yards turn left again away from the road, down a flight of steps between

The Stone Globe, Durlston Castle

two modern blocks of flats. The path now wanders through some overgrown woodlands. The woods have been cut back a little recently, and a number of viewpoints give glimpses out to sea, towards the Isle of Wight.

As the path arrives at Durlston, keep straight ahead (another path leaves to the right, to the car parking area), and almost immediately you will reach Durlston Castle. Turn left, and walk down the right-hand side of the Castle, past the cafeteria until you reach the stone globe.

The stone globe is, along with Corfe Castle and Old Harry Rocks, a familiar picture on postcards. It was constructed in 1887 in Mowlem's yard at Greenwich from 15 pieces of Portland stone held together by granite dowels, and is estimated to weigh about 40 tons.

The globe has weathered relatively well, and most of the detail can still be made out. Around it, Burt put up a series of tablets quoting the poets, as well as a blank stone inscribed

"Persons anxious to write their names will please do so on this stone only". Also nearby are old London metal bollards: Swanage has over 100 of them in total, rescued by Burt when they were no longer required in the capital.

Beyond the Globe the coast path continues, with a fine view out to sea. A bracing sea wind often accompanies it, making a pleasant change after the sheltered woodlands of Durlston Bay. Turn right and follow the coast path as it winds along the cliff edge, past the old entrance to the Tilly Whim Caves. The Caves – old stone quarries – are now closed to the public, due to the danger of rock falls, but can be seen behind you as you leave the Durlston estate path and scramble down, and then up, a little valley towards the lighthouse.

The lighthouse at Anvil Point was erected in the early 1880s. It is now open to the public, normally from 11am to an hour before sunset from Easter to September, except when maintenance work is needed, or when there is fog. You can check by phoning Swanage (0929) 422146.

Beyond the lighthouse, the coast path continues enticingly. If you have the time and energy, carry on a little further. Thrift, sea plantain and samphire are among the plants and flowers growing here, and the cliffs are home for many types of sea-birds. Enjoy the sea views along the Purbeck coast, before retracing your steps.

Leave the lighthouse along the tarmac access road for a short distance inland, until a small whitewashed bridge is crossed. Immediately turn sharp left, and scramble up a steep little hillside. The path here may be a little indistinct, but on your left you'll see a stone wall running parallel, about 20 yards away. Follow the wall up the hillside, and make for the gate in it which comes into view ahead of you.

Pass through the gate, and immediately to your right you'll see another gate, leading into a meadow. This is the start of the path

The Lighthouse, Anvil Point

back to Swanage. Enter the meadow (stones set in the wall provide an alternative to the gate), and continue down the right-hand side of the field. Another stone stile takes you out of this field, the path briefly becoming a lane. (At this point you cross one of the nature trail routes laid down for the Durlston Country Park; away to your right is the Country Park information centre).

Follow the track as it passes into a meadow. From now on, there is easy walking back to the centre of Swanage. The town itself comes into view shortly on your right, while over to the left is the pocked ground which denotes former quarrying activity. Keep to the path along the left hand side of a small meadow, leaving the field to follow the lane which runs almost straight ahead.

The track skirts to the right of a smallholding and a modern house, climbing up a slight hill. More new houses appear on the right, and the track briefly becomes tarmac. Carry straight ahead, and in due course Swanage church tower appears, directly ahead.

You emerge into Townsend Road. Drop down to the High Street, and turn right to retrace your steps to the pier. (Before you do, you may want to take the opportunity of exploring the old Mill Pond area, or visiting the Tithe Barn museum, just next to the church).

As you walk back down the High Street, notice the frontage of Swanage's Town Hall, another London souvenir saved by George Burt. This was originally the entrance to the Mercers' Hall in Cheapside, London, and dates back to 1670. Across the road from the Town Hall is George Burt's former residence, Purbeck House, which not surprisingly has its own curiosities – including statues from London's Royal Exchange, and stone balustrades from the old Billingsgate Market.

6. Langton Matravers – Herston – Godlingston – Windmill Knap – Langton Matravers

Five miles of peaceful country walking between Langton Matravers and Swanage, taking 2 – 3½ hours.

Starting point Langton Matravers church. Park nearby, in a side road. Buses run from Swanage, Corfe and Wareham.

Facilities The walk begins and ends close to the Kings Arms pub (morning coffee and snacks, as well), and White's the bakers, who also do tea and coffee. Herston, a third of the way along the route, offers the Globe pub, shops and a fish and chip shop. Toilets.

Problems Can be muddy in parts. The route is generally waymarked, though the paths are not as well-walked as others in this book.

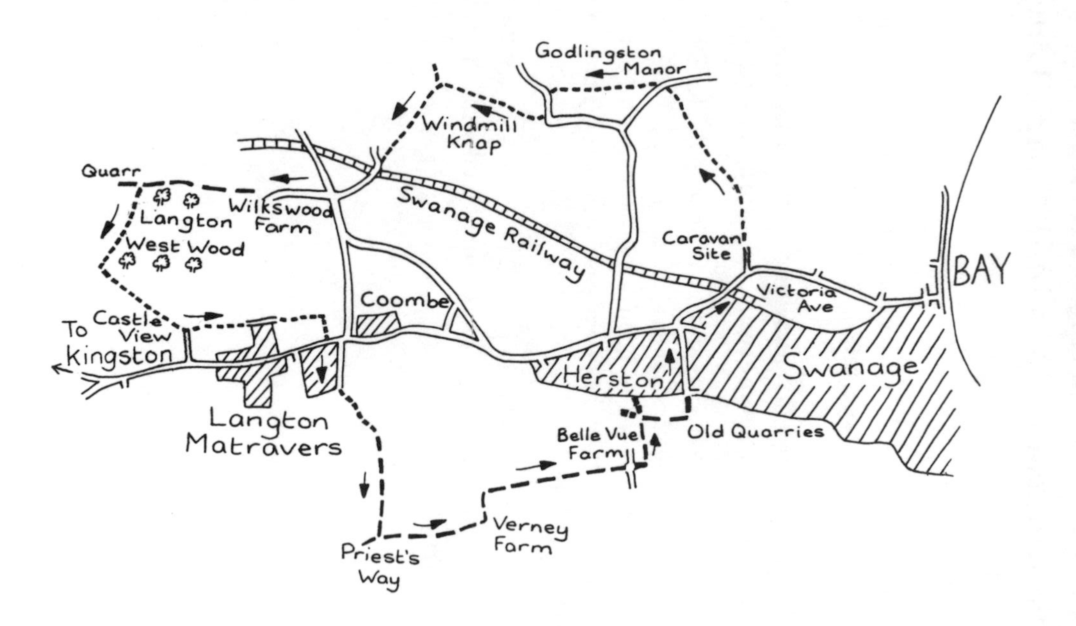
Godlingston Manor
Windmill Knap
Quarr
Wilkswood Farm
Langton West Wood
Swanage Railway
Caravan Site
BAY
Victoria Ave
Coombe
To Kingston
Castle View
Swanage
Herston
Langton Matravers
Belle Vue Farm
Old Quarries
Verney Farm
Priest's Way

DESCRIPTION

There's nothing dramatically beautiful about Langton Matravers in the way that perhaps there is about some of the other Purbeck stone villages – Worth or Kimmeridge, for example. Langton is strung out, as its name suggests, along a busy road from Swanage, and for many visitors this is all they see, as they drive through on the way to somewhere else.

This is a shame: Langton is an interesting place. Its economy has been – and is still today – focused on the quarrying industry, as the village museum (complete with a little reconstruction of life underground in an old stone mine) makes amply clear. It's worth taking time, on foot, to explore the lanes and drove-ways which run off from the main road, particularly on the north side of the village.

Like Langton itself, there's nothing spectacular about this walk: no wildly dramatic cliff paths or sea views, for instance. There are, however, other pleasures to be had.

For this is the walk for anyone who enjoys rediscovering the old green lanes of England: the half-forgotten routes, which could have become busy tarmac roads, if history had been different. Instead the lanes, now merely farm tracks, footpaths or bridleways, serve as a reminder of how all country roads used to be.

The most well-known of Purbeck's green lanes is the Priests Way, the track which can be followed all the way from Worth Matravers to Swanage. Many centuries ago, Swanage's church was only a daughter chapel to the main church at Worth, and this was the path, so it is said, that the Worth priests took as they walked across to Swanage for their pastoral duties.

The Priests Way near Worth has become just a dusty track, and is not especially pleasant walking. But near Langton it is still a sunken lane, running between high walls and hedges: this is the part of the Priests Way which we reach on this walk, after a short walk out from Langton.

Across the valley, near Godlingston, you will encounter another section of a green lane, this time among the trees along the edge of Windmill Knap. This is enjoyable walking in any season, but particularly so in Spring when the bluebells are out.

And finally, to the north of Langton village, between the old marble quarrying areas of Wilkswood and Quarr, the walk joins up with another green lane, now shrunk to a bridleway. This marks the route which used to be followed by the old road between Swanage and Corfe, now long replaced by the main Valley Road.

In between, the walk takes us across fields on the outskirts of Swanage to one of the most beautiful of Purbeck's mediaeval houses, Godlingston Manor. Godlingston is hidden up a little drive, out of the sight of passing motorists: walkers alone have a chance to appreciate its beauty.

DIRECTIONS

Walk down Langton's main street from the church, passing the Kings Arms. Turn right into The Hyde. Just past the last of the houses, before the road becomes a private drive, turn left up a little path. Almost immediately, at a stile, head half-right across a small field making for the far corner. Here, at another stile, turn right and follow a farm track.

The track runs out across a field before turning left, making for the further corner of the field, beside a stile and gate. Beyond the gate, the track continues as a pleasant lane, shortly with dry-stone walls to both left and right. After a few hundred yards, the lane arrives at a T-junction. Turn left, on to the Priests Way.

Follow the Priests Way, a quiet lane running between stone walls, gently downhill. It swings into the corner of a large field, near a new barn. Keep along the right-hand edge of this field, but then bear left, down a second side of the field, ignoring the roadway which continues

The Priest's Way

ahead to Verney Farm. After a short distance, turn right along another little lane, skirting the farm buildings to your right. When this lane swings right, towards some more farm buildings, follow the Priests Way straight ahead: over a stile, across a field, and then over a second stile.

Beyond here the Priests Way is once again hemmed between hedges, first as a lane, and then (when the lane disappears into a field) as a small footpath. Some steps set in a wall take you over into a field close to the buildings of Belle Vue Farm. Carry on through this field, cross a farm lane, and then turn left immediately you have entered the next large field. Follow the well-worn path down the left side of this field past a number of houses (over to the right is one of Swanage's caravan sites). Pass through a gate, and follow the path round to the right.

You have now reached the edge of the new developments at Herston. The path carries on for a few yards along the bottom of a field, before widening and emerging near some houses. At this point turn sharp left, down a narrow path. This shortly brings you to a street of houses. Keep walking down the street, past Herston Church and school, emerging beside the Globe public house.

Cross straight over the High Street, and follow Victoria Avenue towards Swanage for a little way. Shortly after the railway bridge, take the track immediately to the left of the Triangle Garage. When the track continues towards a caravan site, at a cattle grid, turn right over a stream and then immediately left, to find a footpath running along a small grassy hillside. To your left, beyond the stream, are the caravans.

The track leads straight to a stile in the far hedge. In the second field, keep to the left hand edge, continuing to keep the stream to your left. A stile comes into sight in the far corner; however, just as you approach this, a second stile becomes visible, crossing the stream to the left. This is the path you want.

After crossing the stream, the path bends round, following the right-hand edge of another field. In due course, the path turns right, recrossing the stream once more. At this point, make straight ahead, along the right-hand edge of a field, keeping a small drainage ditch to your right. You emerge by way of a stile on to a tarmac road. Cross the road, and take the driveway half left, to walk to Godlingston Manor.

Godlingston is an instantly attractive building. Much of what you can see was built about 1300 – from this time dates the unusual rounded tower, which architectural historians assume must originally have been built as a defensive feature, and most of the main frontage of the house. There have been some changes over the centuries, of course: the windows go back (only) to the early seventeenth century, a time when the rear of the house was extensively rebuilt. Much more recently, in the late 19th century, the east wing (to your right, as you look) was rebuilt after a fire. Godlingston is however no museum piece, but a busy working farm. Nevertheless, it is supposed to have its own resident ghost, a lady who has been seen walking by the garden wall, and sometimes in the house itself.

Pass the Manor, and walk through the farmyard. Beyond, the path continues ahead, slightly up hill, following the left edge of a field. When this field opens out to your left, head half-left towards a small group of trees. You will emerge at a gate giving on to the road from Godlingston to Knitson.

Turn left, following the road for a few yards. When the road swings abruptly to the left, turn sharp right, heading along an old green lane. Cut across the very edge of a large field, used in summer for camping, before climbing a stile into a little wooded area. The old green lane continues, with the hill of Windmill Knap to your left, and a pasture to your right.

Windmill Knap was indeed the site of an old windmill, but according to local tradition its history goes back further, for this is said to be the location of one of three lodges built for King John's use when he was hunting in Purbeck. Another hunting lodge is supposed to have been on Creech Barrow.

When the old lane finally peters out, continue for a few yards until you reach a hedge. Turn left, over a stile, and head down the right-hand side of a large field, with the buildings of New Barn farm directly below in the valley. The path follows the field edge, eventually becoming another sunken lane, before finally a track takes you up to the right to emerge at the farm buildings. Turn left on to the by-road, and follow it down under the railway bridge to the main Swanage-Corfe road.

At the main road, keep straight ahead into the no-through road opposite. Follow the road; shortly the tarmac gives out, and the road bends to the left. Almost immediately, you will see a bridleway sign, pointing off half right.

Take this path. Once more, you are following an old green lane. Keep straight ahead, along first a track and then a path (the track swings right into a field). This is one of the most pleasant sections of the walk, through bracken and woodland, with views to the right down towards Harmans Cross and beyond.

Although there are no obvious signs from the path, this area was for generations the area where Purbeck marble was quarried. The marble, a particularly hard intractable limestone, outcrops only in a narrow band along the hillside. The Romans quarried it near here, at Wilkswood. Later, in mediaeval times, considerable quantities of Purbeck marble were required for many of the great cathedrals, including Salisbury Cathedral and Westminster Abbey. Anyone who has tested the stone's hardness can only have tremendous admiration for the skills of the mediaeval masons who shaped and carved it with such apparent ease. The marble was taken to Corfe Castle, where some of the working of the stone took place, before being transported across the heath to Ower on the edge of Poole Harbour, for loading on to boats.

The bridlepath crosses a footpath, and leads into the edge of Langton West Wood, before finally emerging by some farm buildings at Quarr Farm. Turn left at the first wooden hut through a farm gate, keeping straight across a large field. At the opposite side, a stile takes you into a second field. This is the place to turn round, to get a good view of the attractive stone-built farmhouse.

Quarr means 'quarry' in the local dialect, another reminder of the marble industry. Quarr was reported as supplying marble during the building of Winchester Cathedral. The main part of the farmhouse dates from the eighteenth century, though parts of an earlier seventeenth century house are incorporated into it.

Keep directly across the second field, aiming for the edge of the wood, which has crept back towards the path here. Just beyond the wood, some stone steps in the wall will take you over into a large meadow. There is a choice of paths here: your path heads off half-right, making for Castle View, the group of cottages visible in the distance.

As you approach the cottages, keep them to your right, and emerge through a gateway between a stone barn and a garage. Almost immediately, turn left over a stile into another field. Once more, keep straight across the centre of another large field: ahead, a small gap in some trees marks the site of the next stile. There are wonderful views from here, down to the sea at Swanage, and back along the valley to Corfe Castle.

From the stile, cross directly over a much smaller field to arrive beside a house. Carry straight ahead, along a track beside playing fields towards some more houses. The track shrinks to become just a flagged stone path between stone walls, with houses on both sides, then crosses a road, and continues as a narrow track beside another house before emerging at the edge of a large field. Carry straight ahead, keeping the stone wall to your right. Just before the wall bends out, find a stile into a tiny passageway (the Purbeck word is 'drong') to your right. The drong takes you back, beside Langton churchyard, to the starting point for the walk.

7. Worth Matravers – Dancing Ledge – Seacombe – Winspit – Worth Matravers

An easy four mile walk of 1½ – 2½ hours from Worth Matravers to the coast at Dancing Ledge, and then back along the cliff path to the old quarrying areas at Seacombe and Winspit.

Starting point Worth Matravers village. Park in the visitors car park, on the road from Kingston near the Square and Compass pub. Occasional buses from Swanage, Langton, Corfe and Wareham.

Facilities The Square and Compass is a delightful old Purbeck stone pub, a village local which is also welcoming to visitors. The Worth Tea Rooms provide lunches and teas, including perhaps the best Dorset Cream Teas in Purbeck.

Problems The paths are easy and well marked, and should present few difficulties. The path from Eastington to Dancing Ledge is, at the time of writing, not shown on Ordnance Survey maps.

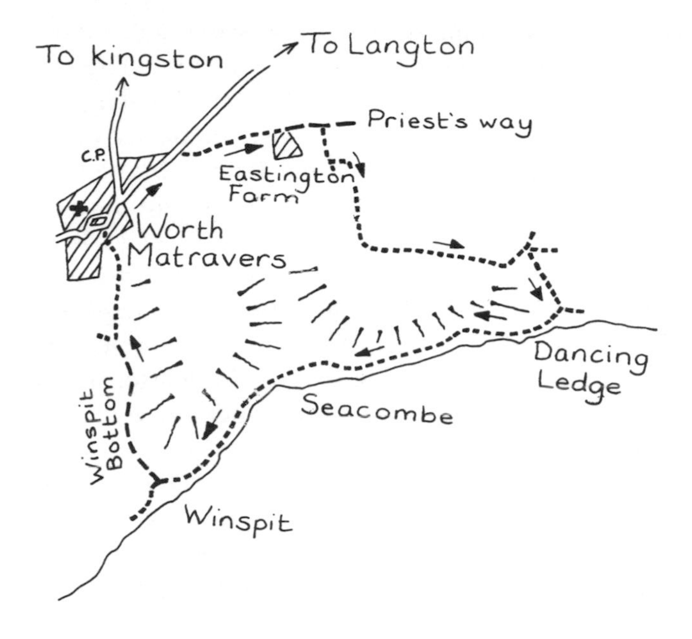

DESCRIPTION

One of the delights of Dancing Ledge must be its name. It is the sea that does the dancing, throwing up foam along the smooth flat ledge that juts out into the English Channel. On summer days, it's a pleasant place to sit and relax, watching the passing shipping in one direction and the passing hikers on the Dorset coast path in the other.

More strenuous activity is also possible. A rocky pool in the ledge offers an unusual opportunity for swimming, having originally been blasted out of the rock for the use of schoolboys from a school in Langton Matravers. For a time their 'swimming pool' was carefully protected from the public by an iron grille. Now it's available to anyone who's brave enough to face the cold, and doesn't mind sharing the water with a few little crabs. (Personally, I've never yet gone beyond paddling!)

Dancing Ledge began life as a quarry, but it's been a favourite place for excursions for generations. On at least one occasion in the past, it lived up to its name. William Masters Hardy, a Swanage builder and knowledgeable local historian, wrote a classic book of reminiscences of *Old Swanage, or Purbeck Past and Present*, which was published in 1910. He recounts one particular picnic at Dancing Ledge, attended by the massed ranks of the Swanage Brass and Reed Band. After lunch at one o'clock ("a plentiful repast, consisting of a lobster tea, salad and liquid refreshments"), the band struck up, and dancing took place until the party finally returned to Swanage at six.

Dancing Ledge can only be reached by walking, and traditionally it's approached from Langton Matravers. Cars can be driven down Durnford Drove, a rather cheerless and almost surburban road, as far as Spyway Farm, and then it's a shortish walk across fields to the coastline.

My route, from Worth Matravers, is a little further, but in my opinion well worth the extra effort. The path from Langton and Spyway is pleasant enough, but the path from Worth is a real treat. And starting from and finishing at Worth provides an excuse for a cream tea at the Worth Tea Rooms or a drink in the Square and Compass.

The National Trust now own much of this land, and they have added considerably to the pleasures of walking here by creating several new paths, and by erecting neat stone waymarks. The path followed in this route from Eastington Farm to Dancing Ledge is one of these new National Trust paths, and may not be on your map. I walked it for the first time while researching this book – and immediately decided it had to be included: one of the best walks in this part of Purbeck.

DIRECTIONS

Leave Worth village by heading back along the Langton road, past several houses. Just beyond the Newfoundland Close development, a footpath sign points you right over a stile into a small field. Take this path, cross almost immediately the driveway to Abbascombe house (two more stiles), and then head across the next field, aiming for the far corner. A stile takes you into another much larger field, dropping down to the right into a little valley. Keep on the brow, however, and also avoid the track through a gap in a stone wall ahead. Instead, stay to the left of this wall, to arrive in due course at a gateway. Keep ahead along a track, passing to the left of Eastington Farm.

You are now on the Priests Way, the old route followed in mediaeval times when the priests at Worth serviced a daughter church at Swanage (see the introduction to the previous Walk). Eastington Farm itself dates back to the seventeenth century, one of several stone-built farmhouses in Purbeck which have survived from this time. Several of Eastington's original round-headed windows remain in place.

Turn right off the Priests Way at the first gate past Eastington Farm. A National Trust stone conveniently confirms the spot. Cross the next field, and go through a gateway at the end. There is now a choice of paths. One track disappears down the valley to Seacombe. Our path, however, turns left, and skirts round the brow of the hill, parallel to a boundary stone wall. Another stone indicates that Dancing Ledge is 1¼ miles away.

From the path, the strip lynchets can be clearly seen on the hillside opposite. Strip lynchets were mediaeval field systems designed to level off the hillsides and make crop-growing easier, and are visible in several parts of Worth parish.

The path turns sharp left, and once past a stile, you enter a large field, which falls away right towards the sea. Carry along the edge of this field, keeping the stone wall to your left. There are wonderful views over the English Channel: even better, the path conveniently slopes downhill all the way.

Keep alongside the wall into a second field, crossing a footpath from Acton to the sea which is marked by another N.T. stone. When finally the field ends, take the stile in the corner, and turn inland for a short way.

After only a hundred yards or so, you will reach another way-mark stone and stile. Turn right into the neighbouring field, and then double back, finding the path which heads diagonally down the hillside. (Ignore both the track along the field top, and another track heading straight down the hill). The path leads directly down to Dancing Ledge. If you want to visit the Ledge, cross out of the bottom field, and follow the path down to the sea.

As well as its function as a quarry, Dancing Ledge played a useful role in another former element of the local economy. Once again, William Masters Hardy's book is worth quoting (he is describing the years around 1830): 'As one time there were a number of people in Langton and the neighbourhood well known to be great smugglers. One dark night in December they were expecting a cargo of tubs in at Dancing Ledge. The ganger and his men were all on the Ledge watching for their craft. They had not long to wait before she came. They got the tubs ashore all right, and away went the boat to sea again in the darkness.'

However, then came the question of what to do with the haul. Overnight the barrels were left at Spyway barn, guarded by the local bull which had conveniently been allowed to roam free that night. Next morning the smugglers moved the cargo to a more secure, and more unlikely, refuge – in Langton church: 'Most of the smugglers' hiding places had become

Napoleonic Cannon at Cannon Cove

well known to the Coastguards,' explains Hardy. 'Another had to be found somewhere. One of the head [smugglers] thought he knew a first-rate place, which was over the ceiling of the church in the apex of the roof . . . reached by going up inside the tower. This new place was used for smuggling for a long time before it was discovered.'

The coast path runs along the south side of the field which you crossed when reaching Dancing Ledge. Follow it along the cliff edge towards Seacombe, a mile away.

At Seacombe, turn inland up the valley for a few hundred yards, following the dusty track. Finally, when the last of the quarried areas

Seacombe Quarries

is past, turn left up some steps, to continue along the coast path. (At this stage, as an alternative, you could save half a mile or so by carrying on up the valley towards Worth Matravers, though the footpath is not particularly interesting).

At the top of the steps, the path turns left, and quickly rejoins the cliff-side. This time the boundary fence is on the right, with the cliff directly to the left (though at one stage there's a deep quarry on the right as well). There are fine views back towards the lighthouse at Anvil Point, and this is a good place to see just how extensive the cliff quarries were along all this stretch of coastline. Seacombe and

Winspit are two of the largest old quarries, both with honeycombs of tunnels extending back from the sea, but the sites of others, long unworked, are marked by the strange square-cut caves in the cliffs which can be clearly seen from the coast path.

At Winspit, the path skirts the quarry, before dropping down to the valley. The stone roof of Winspit Cottage is visible as you climb down the steps.

Winspit Cottage was the home of the last of the quarrymen in this area, William Jeremiah Bower (Billy Winspit to everyone locally), who was almost eighty when he died in 1966. His father, grandfather and great-grandfather had also been quarrymen.

Winspit was one of the places where stone from the coastal quarries was once winched into small boats brought in-shore for the purpose, which then had to be rowed back around Anvil Point and Peveril into the relative safety of Swanage Bay. It was a hazardous exercise, as William Masters Hardy makes clear: 'It often happened that, when the boat was hauled in under the perpendicular and overhanging cliffs . . . and made fast for loading the stone, which was lowered down by means of tackle and cranes, from 90 to 100 feet above, it would sometimes slip from the tackle, and, dashing down with tremendous force, would perhaps just miss the heads of the leading men in the boats, and plunge into the water, almost overwhelming the stone mariners with seas of trouble they were not seeking.'

The boats themselves, heavily laden with stone, could be very unseaworthy: 'It was only frantic and prolonged efforts at bailing and energetic verbal encouragement from the sailors on the vessels close by that would save the boat, crew and stone from sinking and being lost in the depths of that forbidding coast. But sometimes such was the callousness which familiarity with danger bred in the onlookers during such exciting times that instead of rowing to and assisting the puffing and sweating bailers, these humourous sailors would simply goad on the poor toilers by laughing at them and cracking jokes at their expense'.

From Winspit, follow the track back up the valley towards Worth. At a divide in the road, take the right turn to Worth. The track shrinks to a path, which shortly takes you over a stile into a grassy field. Bear diagonally left, following the well-worn path in the turf. Two more stiles take you finally back to the cottages at Worth village.

8. Worth Matravers – Winspit – St Aldhelm's Head – Chapman's Pool – Worth Matravers

A four mile clifftop walk from one of Purbeck's most attractive villages, taking 1½ – 2½ hours.

Starting point Worth Matravers village. As for Walk 6, park in the visitors car park, on the road from Kingston near the Square and Compass pub. Occasional busses from Swanage, Langton, Corfe and Wareham.

Facilities The Square and Compass pub; Worth tea-rooms; village shop (see introduction to previous walk for more about Worth village).

Problems The footpaths are easy to find and well-walked. Watch out for the stiff climb down, and then up, on the stretch from St Aldhelm's Head to Chapman's Pool.

DESCRIPTION

The maps give you a choice of saints, but there is no doubt that the headland south of Worth Matravers is rightfully named after St Aldhelm, who in the seventh century converted the heathen Purbeck people to Christianity. A surprising amount is known about him: he was born in 735 and was the first Bishop of Sherborne. Several of Purbeck's churches, it is said, may be built upon the sites of original churches established by Aldhelm. (The little chapel at St Aldhelm's Head itself is not quite so ancient, dating merely from the twelfth century).

You don't need to be a specialist in Saxon or Norman church history to enjoy this walk, however. From Winspit to Chapman's Pool is coastal walking all the way, with views to be enjoyed both eastwards towards Durlston and Dancing Ledge and then – once the headland is turned – to the west, towards Kimmeridge, Worbarrow and the distant shape of the Isle of Portland.

The coast path along Purbeck's south coast is deservedly popular with walkers. In fact, it makes up a section of the South-West Peninsula long-distance footpath, the longest of the Countryside Commission's official national routes. The South-West Peninsula path begins just a few miles away, at Poole Harbour, at the northern tip of Studland Bay. It ends 520 miles later at Minehead in Somerset.

In between, walkers have the chance to relish at their leisure the cliffs and coastline of four counties. The path crosses from Dorset into Devon near Lyme Regis, then into Cornwall beyond Plymouth, before turning the corner at Lands End, and doubling back up the northern coast, finally reaching the Exmoor National Park, and then at last Minehead.

520 miles takes some planning – so I suggest you leave the full length of the long-distance path for another day, and just make the most of this four mile walk for now.

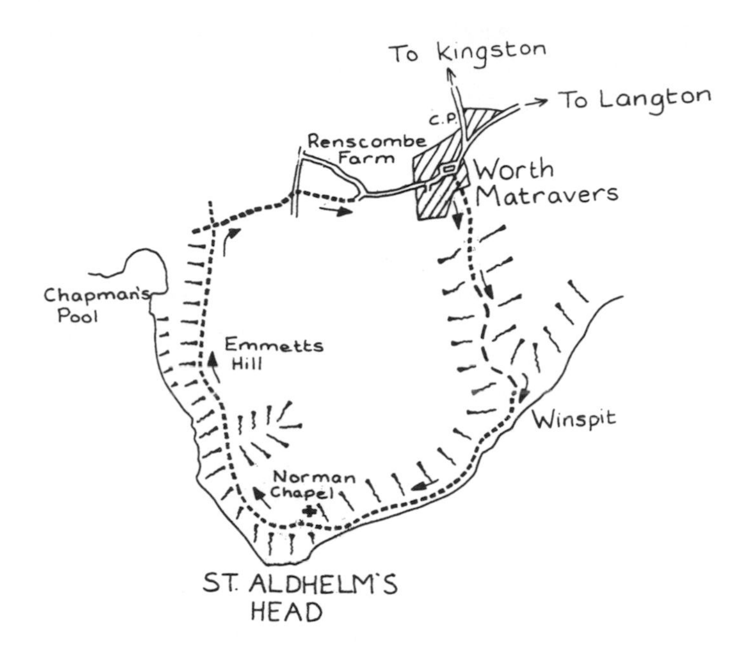

DIRECTIONS

From the centre of the village, follow the footpath signs towards Winspit. The path passes a small row of cottages, London Row, before bearing left into a large field. Cross this field by the well-defined track, over a stile, and follow the track down the valley. An unmade-up road joins from your right; the track continues downhill, hugging the side of the hill while, to your left, runs an overgrown stream.

Shortly after a gate, the track passes to the right of Winspit Cottage (see previous walk). Almost immediately, and before Winspit itself is reached, take a little path to your right, climbing up the side of an old quarry – the stone from here built most of Worth village. The path skirts the very edge of the quarrying area, before reaching the coast proper. There is a fine view down to Winspit, and back along the coast to the lighthouse at Anvil Point, with the old quarries in the cliffs clearly visible all the way back.

The path now hugs the cliff-edge, with the cliffs tumbling away to your left. There are some excellent opportunities to view the sea-birds nesting in the cliffs below (puffins can sometimes be seen along this coastline). Out to sea, rough waters mark the St Aldhelm's Head tidal race.

This is a potentially treacherous stretch of coast, which has claimed its share of shipwrecks. One of the worse was during a wild night in January 1786, when a 785 ton East Indian with 242 people on board, the *Halsewell*, was wrecked near Seacombe. One of the crew managed to clamber up the cliff-side to sound the alarm, and local quarrymen helped to rescue over eighty people from the ship; but a total of 166 men and women lost their lives. Other ships have come to grief on the Purbeck coastline since then but the loss of the *Halsewell* was particularly dramatic and is still talked about today.

As St Aldhelm's Head is approached, the path leaves the sea-edge and begins to climb. After a few more minutes, the roof of a small chapel comes into sight. The path swings round past the coastguard lookouts, looking a little precarious on the cliff-edge. The coast path continues beyond the coastguard station, but it is worth walking a few yards inland to visit the Norman chapel.

The isolated chapel of St Aldhelm is a remarkable building, dating back to the late twelfth century. Its square shape is unusual for a religious building: it is believed to have served as a chantry, where priests performed masses for the safety of sea-farers. A local story has it that the chapel was erected by a father who had watched helplessly as his newly-married daughter and her bridegroom were drowned just off the headland. It seems quite possible that, at one time, the roof held a sea-mark to warn others at sea of the dangers of this stretch

St Aldhelm's Chapel

of coast.

The chapel began to fall into disrepair, and was only restored as a chapel in the nineteenth century. However, the carved dates on the central pillar – including 1629, 1665 and several sets of initials – are thought to be genuine. A superstition which continued well into living memory had it that it was lucky to make a wish while dropping a pin into one of the holes in this pillar. The chapel is still used for occasional church services, including in recent years a communion service at dawn on Easter Day.

Continue from St Aldhelm's Head along the coast path. As the path turns the corner of the headland, a fine view along the coast towards Portland comes into sight. The impressive white cliff in the distance is at Worbarrow, where the chalk Purbeck hills drop into the sea. A little nearer, providing an obvious geological contrast, is the ragged limestone edge of Gad Cliff, also inside the Army ranges. Coming back along the coast from Gad, the low shaley cliffs of Kimmeridge, with the thin finger of the Clavell Tower, can be seen, as can the high land of Swyre Head, and nearer still, Houns Tout Cliff.

The path drops sharply, and then immediately climbs again. This is a stiff climb, with a wooden handrail proving useful in wet weather. Continue along the edge of the cliff, beside a large pasture. In due course, the semi-circle of Chapman's Pool comes into sight directly below the path. A few wooden boathouses can also be seen at the water's edge.

Cross a stile into a grassy hillside, which slopes down on your left towards the sea. Keep the stone wall to your right, and carry on until Chapman's Pool is behind you, and a small waymarking stone is reached. This is the place to turn left, and double back down the hill if you want to visit Chapman's Pool itself.

Over a quarter of a century has passed since the summer of 1961 when a wild grey seal arrived unexpectedly at Chapman's Pool, and stayed from May to November. The extraordinary story of 'Sammy' as the media decided to call him, his encounters with local people and holidaymakers and the desperate attempts to prevent one family from having him shot have been told in *Seal Summer*, a classic animal story recounted by Nina Warner Hoole. She got to know the seal so well during the summer that they frequently went swimming together in the waters around the cove.

At the waymarking stone, turn right (or, if you are returning from Chapman's Pool cross the coast path and keep straight ahead), cross the stile, and follow a track through the first field. The houses of Worth village are directly ahead. Once in the second field, the path runs at a slight angle away from the right-hand stone wall, finally bending round to the left to emerge at a stile on to the road to St Aldhelm's Head.

Cross the road, and immediately find another path, running onwards on the left edge of a large field towards a large green silo. You will emerge shortly beside a farmyard; turn half-left, and then right, to follow the tarmac road back to Worth village.

9. Corfe Castle – Kingston – Puddle Mill – Church Knowle – Cocknowle – Corfe Castle

This five mile walk comprises three distinct parts, and three different types of countryside: the common land between Corfe and Kingston, the rolling farmland running down to the Corfe river at Puddle Mill, and a final stretch along the Purbeck ridgeway between Cocknowle and Corfe. Allow 2 – 4 hours.

Starting point Corfe Castle village. Park in the West Street car park (signs from market place). Corfe is also on the main Wareham-Swanage bus route.

Facilities There's a chance to break this walk both at Kingston and at Church Knowle. Kingston: Scott Arms pub; Kingston Tea Room and shop. Church Knowle: New Inn pub and Purbeck Cottage restaurant; shop.

Problems It would be unfair not to admit that you may find the path overgrown, particularly in high summer, between Kingston and Puddle Mill. The path across Corfe Common can be a little muddy; the final ridgeway path, as you would expect, poses no difficulties.

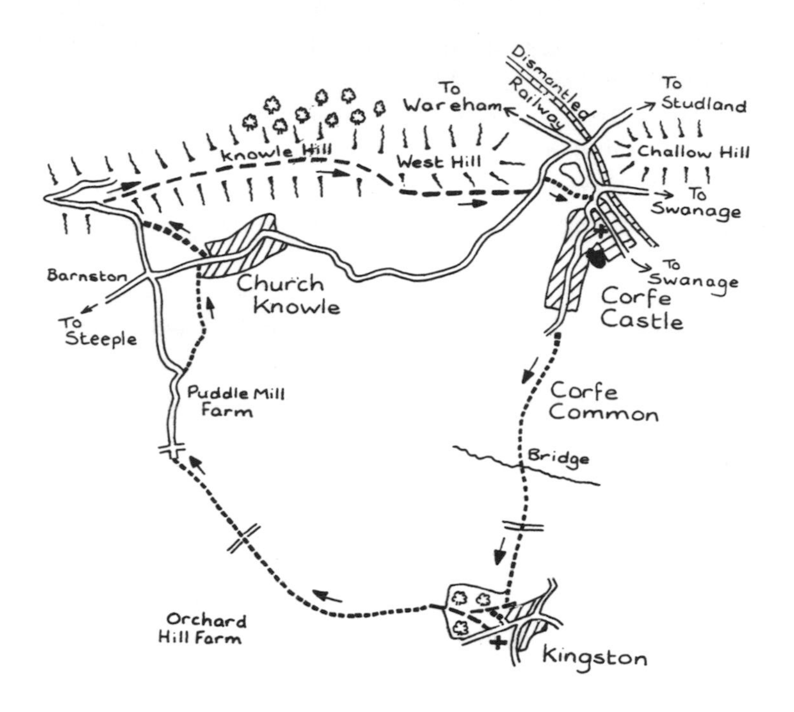

DESCRIPTION

The temptation when starting a walk from Corfe is to make for the Purbeck Hills; and the temptation when walking near Kingston is to head straight for the coast. Perhaps that's why the peaceful valley of the River Corfe, stretching between Tyneham in the west and Corfe Common, where the river turns north on its way through the gap in the hills to Poole Harbour, isn't explored more often.

But this walk has variety, good views – and two well-situated pubs. When I first tried to walk from Kingston to Puddle Mill several years ago, the task became an ordeal – the paths were non-existent and barbed wire was everywhere. The paths in the Corfe valley still aren't as well walked as they deserve to be, but work has been done to make things a little easier. The problem is no longer the lack of stiles or waymarks – it's what's between the stiles which can cause difficulties. Be prepared for some stretches where the undergrowth can be high.

Kingston church is the dominant landmark on this walk. It is in fact the second church which Kingston has had – the old Church still stands, though it is now a holiday centre. It was not grand enough, however, for the third Earl of Eldon who in the 1870s commissioned the eminent architect George Edmund Street to build a more handsome edifice. St James's has been described as a miniature cathedral, and – like the mediaeval cathedrals – much use was made in it of Purbeck marble. An old quarry near Blashenwell Farm on Corfe Common was opened specially to provide the material.

The walk begins with a very different architectural treat – a walk along the length of Corfe's West Street, once the main road from the village to Swanage and south Purbeck, and the centre of mediaeval marble trade. The marble would be dragged here, before being shipped from Ower on the edge of Poole Harbour. Underneath West Street, so they say, are perhaps ten feet of stone chippings, remaining as a reminder of the huge quantity of marble and stone which was stored and worked here.

DIRECTIONS

Walk down West Street from Corfe's market place, until the houses and the road stop abruptly at a turning circle. Go through the gate on to Corfe Common. Just to your left, you will see a footpath sign to Kingston. Follow this path over marshy ground, as it turns slightly to the right up a rise before reaching a small brow. From the barrow near here, you will be able to see Kingston church, and the fields and farmhouses in the valley below you.

Make straight down the hill, until the edge of the common is reached at the bottom. There is another signpost and a new kissing gate here. Follow the path over a stream, across a water meadow, and into an irregularly shaped field. Follow the yellow arrow diagonally across part of this field, picking up the edge of the field shortly. You now enter a wonderful shady lane between two fields. Keep to the left of the next two fields, passing West Lynch farm a short distance away on your right. At the next stile, follow the path across the middle of a meadow, almost directly towards Kingston church tower.

The path now enters woodland. Turn right on to a track, and then immediately left, past a row of cottages. Turn right up some old stone steps into a little alley which will take you to the centre of Kingston village.

Kingston is an estate village, the estate being that of Encombe house, a fine country house half a mile away in a secluded valley near the coast. The pub, the Scott Arms, records the family name: John Scott was a successful politician, who when he became Lord Chief Justice in 1799 was made first Lord Eldon, and who bought the Encombe estate in 1807. The estate remains in the Scott family today.

Long before Scott, however, Kingston really did belong to the King, or at least to the royal house of Wessex. Records report that it was given by a certain King Edred to the abbess

Stone Pump, Kingston

of Shaftsbury in 948, who also acquired the 'right of wreck', the valuable right to salvage anything wrecked or washed upon the cliffs nearby.

Turn right, passing the church and some more stone cottages. Just after the last cottages, take the woodland track running off diagonally to your right. Keep straight on until the wood finishes, then leave the track you are on, taking the stile on your left, and following the path at an angle through the first field to a second stile which is clearly visible.

Cross the next field at an angle, aiming for the long boundary hedge at the top of the rise. It's a long field, and can be hard going when the crops are high; but the views down to Corfe Castle and Poole Harbour beyond fully make up for it. At the end of the field, cross a makeshift stile, and follow an overgrown path between two fields for a few yards. Then clamber up to your left, and follow the edge of the field, keeping the nettles and undergrowth to your right. Carry on along the edge for a second field, before dropping back into the undergrowth to your right, to emerge a few yards later at a stile.

Keep straight ahead, this time along the left edge of a field, bounded a few feet away by a stone wall. Orchard Hill farm is a little way off to the left, while down in the valley Church Knowle is clearly in sight. Leaving this field by yet another stile, keep almost straight ahead across a larger field, ignoring the farm track sharp right down the hill. Almost straight ahead, in the middle of a long boundary fence, you should be able to see a stile.

Once over this stile, head down the hill to another stile, slightly to your right. Once over this next stile, turn diagonally left. You are aiming for the bottom left corner of the field, where a row of tall trees begins. From here, follow the path over another stile, along a field edge, and then into an overgrown lane.

You emerge on to the unclassified road between Church Knowle and Kimmeridge. Keep straight ahead, until you reach Puddle Mill farm.

Barnston manor is just ahead of you, and to your left. Another of Purbeck's delightful manor houses, Barnston was built in the late thirteenth centry, and extended in Elizabethan times when a two-storey bay was added to the south front.

Cross the Corfe river, and immediately enter the field on your right, through a metal gate. Cross this field diagonally, finding a little stile at the opposite corner, among some trees. (The old boundary with the adjacent field has been taken up). Keep left through the next field (which is one of the pastures used by the Church Knowle Animal Sanctuary), and cross the final meadow, aiming just to the left of the last cottage. You are now in Church Knowle village.

The Animal Sanctuary was set up in 1968 by Margaret Green, and is now a popular place for children to visit. In all there are thirty-three acres of grassland, providing a home for many elderly donkeys, horses, goats – and cats. There is also an aviary where wild birds who have suffered injury can be looked after, before being released back to the wild.

Turn right on reaching the main road, and almost immediatey find the waymarked arrow on your left. After two small fields, aim across the next larger field, making not for the gap in the top hedge used by the farm track, but one slightly to its left. Once again, you will find this waymarked. Cross the next field, aiming directy for the cottage which is now in sight

When you reach the road at Cocknowle, follow the road up the hill, ignoring the first footpath waymarked on your right. After a few more yards, a wooden bridleway sign is reached. Turn right here, and enjoy the wonderful views of both sides of the ridgeway. The field boundaries which you have walked between Kingston and Puddle Mill are clearly visible across the valley.

The views over the heathland quickly disappear, as the path drops slightly from the hill brow, though there are compensating views behind you towards Tyneham and Worbarrow. Follow the bridleway,

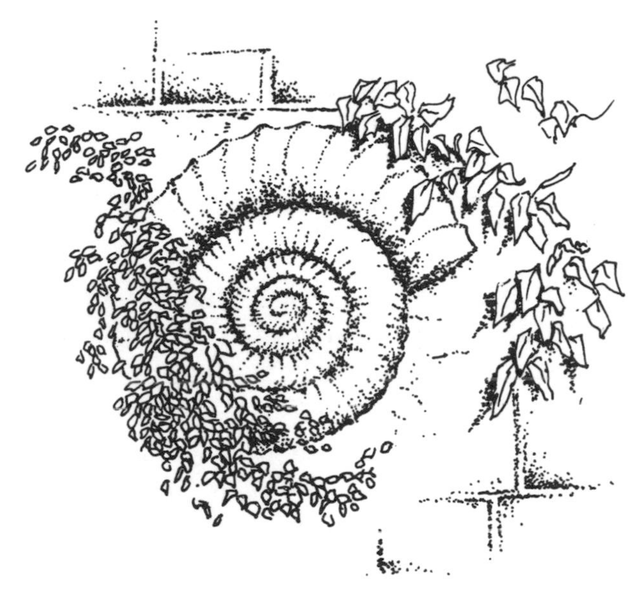

Ammonite in wall, Church Knowle

through a gate (ignoring the stile to its right, which offers another route back to Church Knowle). There are views down to Church Knowle church, which dates from the thirteenth century, lying below you.

The track gradually becomes a path, and suddenly drops down the hillside, at a sharp angle. Follow this path for the remaining half mile until the Corfe-Church Knowle road is reached, just by the Corfe river bridge.

Cross the bridge. You can now follow a little surfaced path around the side of Corfe Castle, until you emerge finally in the village itself.

10. Kingston – Houns Tout – Coast Path – Swyre Head – Kingston

A four mile 1½ – 3 hour walk from Kingston to the coast and back, encircling Encombe House.

Starting point Kingston. Buses run from Swanage, Corfe and Wareham. If driving, carry on through Kingston village and church. A car park has been provided for you, just past the private drive to Encombe House.

Facilities Kingston's pub, the Scott Arms, provides food as well as drinks, and is popular with visitors. Just up the road, the Kingston Tea Rooms provides home-made Dorset Cream Teas – recommended.

Problems The coast path can, in some weather conditions, be a little slippery. There is also quite a steep scramble up to Swyre Head. Otherwise, this walk should provide few problems.

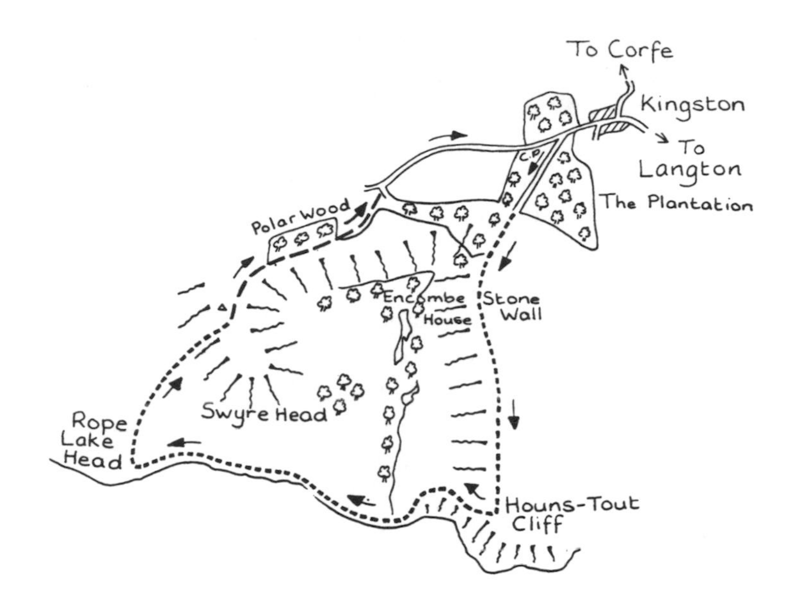

DESCRIPTION

This may very well be the breeziest walk in the book. The wind can whip along the hill-brow above Encombe House, and is always stronger once the coast itself is reached, high up on the cliff edge at Houns Tout. Good for blowing away the cobwebs, certainly; perhaps not quite so advisable on a very windy day.

The walk however describes a circle around one of the most sheltered corners of Purbeck, the quiet valley of Encombe, which has sometimes been described as the 'Golden Bowl'. Encombe House itself is perhaps Purbeck's most architecturally impressive country house. Although it lies in the landscaped parkland below you for much of the walk, there's only really one opportunity to see it clearly, and that is from the top of Swyre Head. (Encombe is not currently open to the public).

Encombe House was built about 1770, probably by the then

owner John Pitt, an amateur architect. Architectural scholars all agree that the house is a fine achievement. "At Encombe one can for once see the grandly austere Vanbrughian idiom being used by another architect in an independent-minded and intelligent way", says John Newman in Pevsner's guide to Dorset, adding "An amateur architect has rarely produced a building as powerful as Encombe". From the house, the succession of man-made lakes to the south give the illusion of being an inlet, suggesting that the sea actually laps at the terrace.

The Encombe estate came to John Pitt in 1734, and passed in due course to his son, William Morton Pitt, a cousin of William Pitt the Younger. William Morton Pitt was also an MP, for some thirty-six years, but was more concerned to improve the conditions of working people in Purbeck than to follow a successful career at Westminster. He campaigned against workhouses, and in favour of smallholdings for local cottagers. He opened a rope factory in Kingston, and developed a straw-plait industry in Langton and Corfe, with the idea of providing more local employment opportunities. He sponsored education, and tried to encourage local children to read and write.

In 1807, however, he sold the Encombe estate. It was purchased by John Scott, recently ennobled as Lord Eldon, a politician of a very different political tendency. Eldon was a controversial figure, determined to destroy the ripples of radicalism spreading from the French Revolution across the channel, which he did by suspending Habeas Corpus and controlling the press.

One contemporary journalist wrote that Eldon "seems to be on his guard against everything liberal and humane as his weak side." He was hated by many, including the poet Shelley who launched a venomous attack on him and his government colleagues in the poem 'The Mask of Anarchy'. Using language which would have present-day politicians phoning their lawyers, Shelley wrote:

St James, Kingston

"Next came Fraud, and he had on,
Like Eldon, an ermined gown;
His big tears, for he wept well,
Turned to millstones as they fell;
And the little children, who,
Round his feet played to and fro,
Thinking every tear a gem,
Had their brains knocked out by them."

Eldon remained deeply conservative to his death. At the end of his life, he made the journey from Encombe to the House of Lord to speak against the "dangerous innovation" of the Great Western Railway.

This walk provides a pleasant combination of hill-top and cliff walking, culminating at Swyre Head, at 666 feet the highest point in Purbeck. In Paul Hyland's opinion (I quote from his book *Purbeck, the Ingrained Island*): "Swyre's promontory is Purbeck's sublimest view-point; and there are no tourist attractions here, no signs or exhortations carved in stone, no car park or road." Altogether, therefore, this is a walk offering a great deal of interest and pleasure.

DIRECTIONS

From the Scott Arms, walk through Kingston village past the church and cottages. Shortly afterwards, turn half left along the private drive to Encombe House. (If using the Houns Tout car park, you will emerge directly on to this drive).

Follow the drive for a few hundred yards through a plantation. When the tarmac road bends off to the right towards Encombe House, carry on almost directly ahead, along a smaller path. Shortly after passing a house on your left, you arrive at a stile into a hilltop field.

The path ahead follows the brow of a steep hill. To the left is a stone wall, with views beyond to the coast. To the right, the field falls down steeply to the valley, where Encombe House is well hidden among the trees. Beyond, on the opposite side of the valley, is an obelisk, erected in commemoration of the first Earl of Eldon's brother.

In due course the path continues through two more fields, usually used for grazing sheep. From the third field, a stile leads directly out to the coast, at Houns Tout Cliff, five hundred feet above the sea below.

Houns Tout is a fine viewpoint, and a stone seat has been helpfully placed here for walkers. St Aldhelm's Head is to the left, Worbarrow Bay and Portland in the distance to the right.

Turn right, and immediately the coast path drops down quite steeply. A few hundred yards later, the path arrives at the end of the gwyle (wooded valley) which runs down to the sea from Encombe. Encombe has its private rocky beach, and you can see the steps disappearing down the rocks to your left. There's also a waterfall where the water from the gwyle cascades into the sea.

The coast path however continues up the other side of the stream. The cliffs suffer from quite serious erosion in this area, and rather alarmingly at one stage the barbed wire fence marking the field boundary to the right of the path has been repositioned: the old barbed wire, and the old cliff path, has fallen into the sea.

The path skirts the high ground of Swyre Head to the right (despite its name, Swyre Head is not on the coast), and then drops down to another little stream. (On some days, the spray reaches up to the footpath, and drenches unwary walkers). Beyond the stream, at the first field boundary, turn right at a stile, and begin to head away from the coast.

This stretch of path provides an invaluable link between Swyre Head and the coast (the next walk also uses it). The path is not a recognised right of way, but rather a concession provided to walkers: therefore you won't find it marked on maps.

From the stile keep up the left hand side of a large field. Cross a farm track, and enter another large field, again carrying on up the left edge. A stile leads into a smaller third field, and the path then continues through a gate into a fourth. From now on, follow the right-hand field boundary. The path begins climbing steeply up the side of the hill – but there are compensations in the fine views back to the sea, and to the right over towards Smedmore House, the neighbouring country house to Encombe.

At the hilltop, a stile will take you over into the grassy area surrounding Swyre Head.

The path we want disappears diagonally left, heading for a stone wall. But it's worth stopping briefly first at Swyre Head (cross the stile to your right, to climb the barrow) to admire the view. Swyre

Head offers the best glimpse so far of Encombe House, down in the valley below.

The path back from Swyre Head to Kingston cuts across the grass, and quickly becomes a well-worn track in the turf. Follow the wall past Polar Wood, along the opposite side of the valley from the one taken at the start of this walk. Once past the wood, the track swings left, away from the brow, through the middle of a large field. The top of Kingston church can just be seen above the trees. When a tarmac road is reached, beside a sheep fold, turn left, and then immediately right, and follow the country road back to Kingston.

11. Kimmeridge – Smedmore Hill – Swyre Head – Coast Path – Kimmeridge Bay – Kimmeridge

A lovely hill walk combined with a fine stretch of the coast: altogether about four miles and taking from 1½ – 3 hours.

Starting point Kimmeridge village. Park in the quarry car park above the village. (The entrance is on the left, just past the junction with the Bradle/Puddle Mill by road, and before the village is reached). No public transport.

Facilities Kimmeridge village offers a cafe and tea-room adjoining the Post Office and village stores. Toilets at Kimmeridge Bay.

Problems Generally, a very straightforward route. The hill down from Swyre Head can be a little slippery.

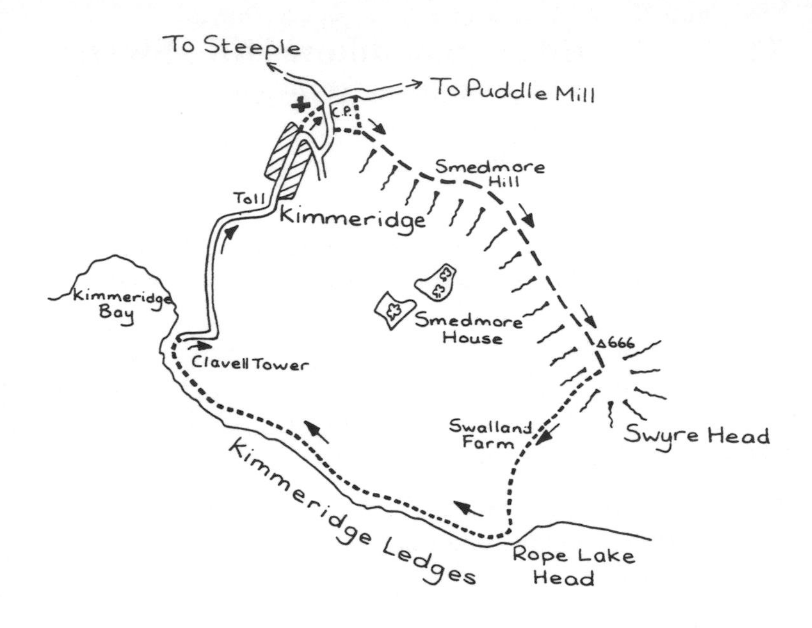

DESCRIPTION

Geologically, the short stretch of coast near Kimmeridge Bay offers a contrast to other parts of Purbeck. In fact the technical term for the kind of rock formation found here, 'Kimmeridge clay', has ensured that geologists at least have heard of this peaceful Purbeck village.

Peaceful today, certainly, but Kimmeridge has an interesting industrial past. As in other parts of Purbeck, human activity has tried to prise wealth from out of the earth. Here the goal has been not marble, stone or clay but the bituminous shale, known as blackstone.

The story goes back a long way, to Bronze Age times, when Kimmeridge shale was fashioned into ornamental armlets. The Romans developed this industry, carving table-legs and other items from the shale with considerable skill.

There was another flurry of industrial activity in the seventeenth century, when the local landowner Sir William Clavell launched two ultimately disastrous business ventures. His first effort, to extract alum deposits from the shale, seemed initially promising, but he was up against other alum producers who claimed that they alone had authority from the Crown. Undaunted, he tried again, this time developing a glassmaking works, using the local blackstone as fuel. To export the glass, and salt which he was extracting from the sea, he built a large jetty, which one contemporary account describes as a "strong huge peere of Stone, 100 foote highe, and 60 foote broade". Sadly, Clavell was again unlucky, getting enmeshed in litigation and being sent on two occasions to a debtor's prison, before returning to Kimmeridge to rescue his estate. His pier, incidentaly is reported to have been destroyed in a storm in 1745.

His bad luck seems also have have dogged numerous nineteenth century companies who also felt that the blackstone could be commercially exploited. From 1848 onwards, Kimmeridge blackstone was converted, among other things, into varnish, pitch, paraffin wax, dyes, and fertiliser. For a short time, it was made into gas to light the streets of Paris: the problem was that it gave off a very unpleasant smell! Later, another company tried to use it in sewage purification.

It is only in the twentieth century that the wealth beneath Kimmeridge's soil has been successfully tapped. Testing for oil began in the 1930s, and recommenced in the '50s – the results were encouraging. Since the late 1950s BP have operated an inobtrusive, but commercially important, 1800 foot oil well, just to the west of Kimmeridge Bay.

None of this history, however, need concern you, if you are simply interested in finding a peaceful and pleasant place to walk. The combination in this circular walk of the limestone ridgeway path from Kimmeridge village to Swyre Head and the coast path back from Swyre to Kimmeridge Bay provides enough interest by itself.

DIRECTIONS

Find the little track climbing up from the corner of the quarry car park. At the top, the path swings left through some rough ground before reaching a wire fence. At the fence, take the small path running forward, in the space between an overgrown hedge (to your left), and a wire fence (to your right). The path soon leaves the field edge to head a few yards to the left, meeting a substantial farm track. Turn right, and follow the track up the hill.

If the initial climb from the quarry seems a little too difficult, there is an alternative: leave the car-park, turn right, and right again on to the road to Bradle. After passing a second quarry, take the farm track off to your right, and follow it up the hill.

The climb is a little tedious, but at last the brow of the hill is reached. Carry on along the brow, enjoying the view which opens up to the left, down to Church Knowle and Corfe Castle, with the Purbeck Hills beyond disappearing towards Swanage.

The track follows the brow of Smedmore Hill, as it swings round to the right to head towards Swyre Head. Down the hill, to your right, it is possible to get a glimpse of Smedmore Hiuse, nestling among the trees.

Smedmore is another of Purbeck's country houses, dating back to the seventeenth century, though much changed in the middle of the eighteenth century. It's a pleasant place, with lovely gardens, and is normally open to the public once a week during the summer months.

The Smedmore estate lands have not been put up for sale since 1391, when the Clavell family first acquired them. There has, however, been at least one occasion when the future of the estate was in doubt. When the Rev. John Clavell died in

Clavell Tower, Kimmeridge

1833, no will could be found. Under the laws of intestacy Smedmore was all set to pass to his nearest relative, his niece Louisa, and her husband Colonel John Mansel, when three months after the death the Clergyman's former housekeeper unexpectedly produced a will, apparently leaving the property to a neighbouring farmer. The lawyers were brought in, and eventually a jury at Dorchester found in favour of the niece's claim and against the will. Smedmore is today still owned by the Mansel family.

When the farm track turns abruptly left away from the brow, keep straight ahead, entering into a small field, just at the hill brow. Leave this field by a small wooden gate, to emerge on to the open grassland surrounding Swyre Head. This is the highest point in Purbeck: at 666 feet Swyre Head beats the Purbeck Hills by about ten feet.

Just before reaching the stile to the barrow on top of Swyre Head, turn right over another stile, to find the path heading straight down the hill. This is the path also taken in the last walk, in the opposite direction: it is not a right of way and does not appear on maps, but public access is allowed for the time being.

Scramble down the hill into a field, keeping the field boundary to your left. Enter through a gate into a small second field, this time walking on the right-hand side of the field. The route of the path can be seen ahead, curving down towards the sea. Carry on into a third field, over a farm track, and then into a large fourth field, still keeping along the right-hand side of the fields.

You reach the coast path at Rope Lake Head. Turn right, climb up a small rise, and almost immediately you will be able to see the Clavell Tower, high above Kimmeridge Bay.

The Tower drops away from sight again, as the coast path continues round another little headland and over a stream, before it once more returns into view. There are fine views along the coast beyond Kimmeridge, to the limestone outcrop of Gad Cliff and the white chalk of Worbarrow Bay. In due course, the path arrives directly beneath the Clavell Tower.

The Tower sadly looks less impressive close to than it does from a distance. It was erected probably in the late eighteenth or early nineteenth century, and seems initially to have been simply a folly, though it was later used by coastguards. When the coastguards moved to another lookout nearby, the tower gradually deteriorated. The cliff here has suffered from considerable erosion, and the tower is now considered to be unsafe.

From the Tower, follow the steps down the hill to arrive beside the boathouses at Kimmeridge Bay. If you want to visit the beach, carry on straight ahead, through the boat-yard. Otherwise, turn right on to the tarmac road, and follow the road up past the toll booth into Kimmeridge village.

Cottages at Kimmeridge

12. Kimmeridge – Gad Cliff – Worbarrow – Tyneham – Kimmeridge Bay – Kimmeridge

A six mile walk from Kimmeridge village along a beautiful hill-ridge to Worbarrow and the lost village of Tyneham. Allow 2½ – 4 hours.

Note: This walk is across the Lulworth Army Ranges, and access is not always possible. Check the information boards (at various places including Lulworth, Stoborough and Corfe), or telephone the Army on Bindon Abbey (0929) 462721. The footpaths are always open from 9 am on Saturdays to 8 am on Mondays, all day on public holidays and daily throughout August.

Starting point Kimmeridge village. Park in the quarry car park above the village. (The entrance is on the left, just past the junction with the by-road to Bradle and Puddle Mill, and before the village is reached; Walk 11 also begins from this car park). No public transport.

Facilities Toilets in Tyneham, and at Kimmeridge Bay. A cafe and tea-room adjoins the Post Office and village stores in Kimmeridge village.

Problems Very well-marked paths, especially on the Army Ranges. Don't be tempted to stray when on the Ranges. Much of the route is down hill, though there's a short climb out of Tyneham village back to Gad Cliff.

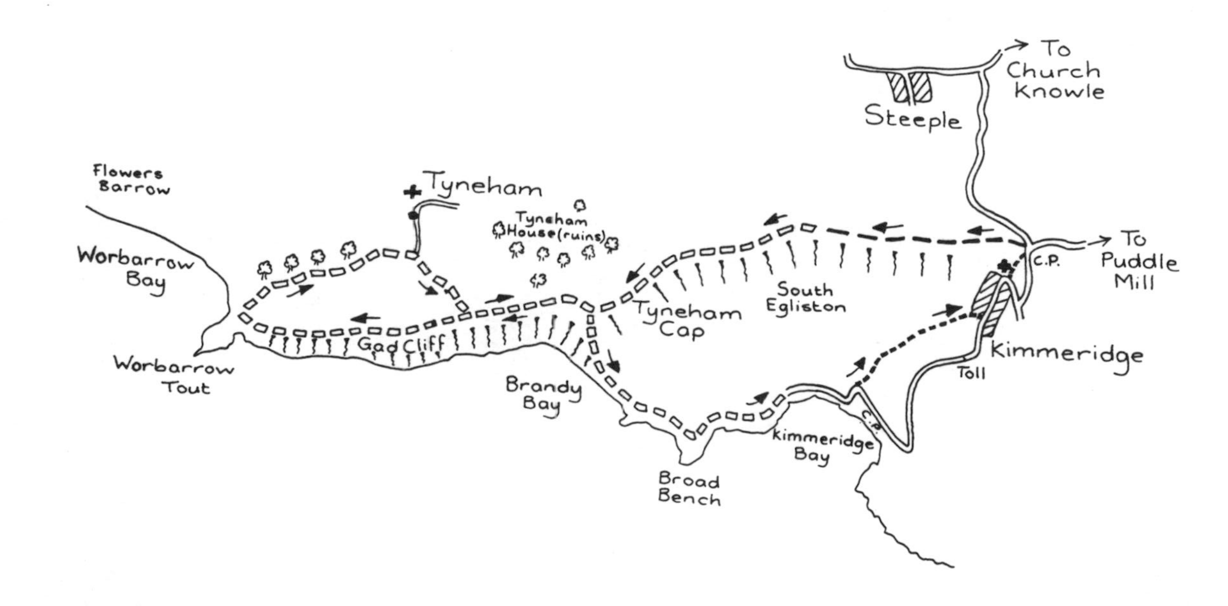
Flowers Barrow
Worbarrow Bay
Worbarrow Tout
Gad Cliff
Tyneham
Tyneham House (ruins)
Brandy Bay
Tyneham Cap
Broad Bench
South Egliston
Kimmeridge Bay
C.P.
Steeple
To Church Knowle
Toll
Kimmeridge
C.P.
To Puddle Mill

DESCRIPTION

'To those who never visited the valley I cannot hope to convey its atmosphere and spirit which were unique and gave to Tyneham its peculiar fascination.

'Descriptions of the ancient house and the surrounding country may indeed bring back to those who loved them something of their quiet, compelling charm, but its quality is inexpressible in words and that elusive quality was the essential Tyneham.'

So begins *Tyneham: A Lost Heritage,* Lilian Bond's powerful and evocative account of family and village life in Tyneham in the early years of the century, written by a member of the family whose roots in Tyneham went back to 1683, the year when Lilian Bond's ancestor, Nathaniel Bond, first purchased the Elizabethan house and estate.

Lilian Bond's book is of general interest to anyone interested in social and rural history. But it has a special poignancy, given that its subject-matter is a village, and a way of life, which disappeared abruptly and by official decree, in a particularly dramatic fashion almost fifty years ago.

Tyneham: A Lost Heritage was first published in 1956, and as the extract I've quoted makes clear, Lilian Bond is writing in the past tense. The story of the Army take-over of the village during the last war is now quite widely known; it was in December 1943, just before Christmas, that the Army requisitioned all the land and houses of the village and evacuated the local people. The land was needed, according to the Army, to extend the nearby Lulworth firing ranges, and would be held for the "duration of the emergency".

When they left, the villagers pinned a modest notice to the church door: "Please treat the church and houses with care; we have given up our homes where many of us lived for generations to help win the war to keep men free. We shall return one day and thank you for treating the village kindly".

Other parts of Purbeck, especially the heathlands bordering Poole Harbour, were taken over by the Army during the war years – and then given back, once peace had returned. But the Army's red flags remained flying over Tyneham. In 1948, the former residents learned that the land was to be compulsorily purchased – and despite angry local allegations of broken promises, and a public enquiry, the sale went ahead.

The houses at Tyneham and Worbarrow, including Tyneham House and the church, were boarded up, and began to disintegrate. As a child I was taken on a number of occasions to visit Tyneham, on those weekend and holiday days when the Army opened the gates on the range and allowed motorists to drive down. It was an intensely depressing place. The cottages, half tumbled down, were completely overgrown, and securely fenced off. Signs warned of unexploded shells. The church, or what could be seen of it, was completely out-of-bounds, and although the track to Worbarrow was opened, it was impossible to explore the countryside or walk along the coast path.

Tyneham House, a listed building, was also out-of-bounds, and – hidden in Tyneham Great Wood – conveniently out of sight as well. Most of the house was Elizabethan, though the south-west wing dated back to mediaeval times. In 1967, the Army decided to demolish it. A few bits and pieces were taken to the County Museum or other country houses, but the demolition lorries took away the rest, leaving only the mediaeval old house, which still survives (still out of public gaze) in a very poor condition.

The destruction of Tyneham House, which many local people felt was wanton vandalism, and the continuing Army occupation of the area led to an upsurge of local protests, and a vigorous campaign was begun by the Tyneham Action Group. For a time, especially when a Royal Commission recommended that the lands should be given up, it seemed that the red flags might come down for good, perhaps to be replaced by National Trust signs.

In the end, the Army remained, but a compromise deal was struck. Public access was allowed much more frequently, and the range walks were opened. The buildings in Tyneham village were spruced up, and the brambles and ivy removed from the churchyard. And so it is today: the ruins are immaculately tidy, the church is open again for visitors (as a museum), and the Army's warning signs more discreet. But the cosmetic tidying of the land can't replace a more fundamental sadness about the way the story has ended.

In the '50s and '60s, despite the destruction and the barbed wire, it still seemed possible that the village might some day live again. Today the loss of Tyneham as a living community seems irrevocable. Tyneham now has only a past – and the conversion of the church and the old schoolroom into museums only serves, in my opinion, to reinforce the presentation of the past as something now out of reach. I would almost rather, I think, still have the brambles and the dereliction.

But undertake this walk, and decide for yourself. The area around Tyneham and Worbarrow has some of the finest and most spectacular scenery in southern England, including the 400 foot high Gad Cliff.

Tyneham village

DIRECTIONS

Leave the quarry car-park, and turn right. Pass the footpath, left, down to Kimmeridge village, but take the next footpath on the left, about twenty yards beyond the road junction. The path hugs the brow of the hill, running ahead along the left-hand edge of a large field; there are fine views down to Kimmeridge village directly below and the bay, while to the right the Purbeck Hills are running parallel, also heading for Worbarrow.

The path enters a second field, and the stone tower of Steeple Church (one of Purbeck's most isolated churches) comes into sight, just a little way back, on the right. A flagpole and gate announces the start of the Army land, and the path continues along the brow, climbing slightly, and now following a wall to the right. Although as the signs remind us there can be unexploded missiles on the Ranges, this stretch of path is at the periphery of the occupied land, and farmers are able to lease land from the Army for arable farming and pasture.

Keep along the brow, until the cliffs of Worbarrow Bay and of Gad come into sight; across the valley, you may notice the cars parked at the viewpoint on Whiteway Hill. Keep the wall on your right, and follow the yellow waymarks. As the coast path comes in on your left, you arrive at a well-positioned stone seat, at a small clump of trees.

This is the Ocean Seat described by Lilian Bond in her book, one of her favourite places when she was a child in Tyneham House. The wall which the path has been following since entering the ranges was the boundary between the Tyneham and South Tyneham (Egliston) estates, both mentioned in the Domesday Book. Many ancient boundaries survive in the field patterns in southern Purbeck.

Climb the stile at Ocean Seat, and turn left, to walk along the edge of Gad Cliff. Tyneham village lies below (a footpath runs off to the right shortly), with the church clearly visible. A little way back up the valley from the village is Tyneham Great Wood, where the ruins of Tyneham House are to be found. (They can be glimpsed in the autumn and winter, when the leaves are off the trees).

Carry on along the edge of Gad Cliff, taking care at the places where the path runs close to the edge. Gad is over four hundred feet high, and sheer. Hunting was stopped in Tyneham after a number of wily foxes had lured fox-hounds over the cliff edge.

The path drops gradually, and as you approach Worbarrow you're rewarded with a fine view down to the tout and the little cove of Pondfield (Punf'ls in local pronounciation). The white chalky cliff of Worbarrow opposite marks the arrival of the Purbeck Hills once more at the coast, twelve or more miles west of Ballard Down.

At the base of Worbarrow Tout turn right, and follow the dusty track up the valley to Tyneham. This is perhaps the least attractive part of the walk, not helped when Army vehicles pass, throwing up dust. However, even before the war, this was a necessary walk for any visitor wanting to get to the sea; cars then, as now, were left at Tyneham.

As you arrive at Tyneham, the path back is on the right, climbing up a slippery hillside back to Gad Cliff. However, if you have time, you may want to turn left to explore what remains of the village.

Near the new public conveniences are the buildings of what was Tyneham Farm, now in relatively good condition again. Lilian Bond describes how the celebrated Dorset Blue Vinney cheese used to be made in the top floor of the dairy house. Rows of the cheese, at different stages of the ripening process, would be stood on well-scrubbed boards. According to Mrs Bond, the smell of the cheese lingered on for years after cheese-making stopped.

From Tyneham take the footpath up the hillside to Gad Cliff and Tyneham Cap, to rejoin the coast path. Turn left, and retrace your steps to the Ocean Seat.

From the seat, leave the brow and take the coast path down the hill, heading for Kimmeridge Bay. The path drops steadily: follow the yellow waymarks, for the path may be rerouted slightly to avoid excessive erosion of the turf.

Kimmeridge Bay lies ahead, but first the path skirts the edges of two smaller bays, Brandy Bay and Hobarrow Bay. The ruins of the farm at South Egliston and of Stickland's Cottage peer out from trees which mark the wooded valley of Egliston Gwyle. The coast path continues, becoming almost a track, and in due course the steps down to Charnel Ledges are passed (these ledges can be reached even when the Range walks are shut). Carry on, until the flagpole and metal gate marks once again the Ranges boundary. Almost immediatey, you'll arrive at the BP pumping station.

One of the Heritage Coast information boards helpfully recounts the whole history of oil exploitation in Kimmeridge. An exploratory bore-hole was sunk in 1936, but it was not until the late 'Fifties that the geologists returned. The pumping jack (or nodding donkey) brings up crude oil from 1790 feet below the cliffs, and the oil is then taken away by road to the Furzebrook railway siding near the Blue Pool, on its way to a refinery in South Wales.

Follow the path a few yards to the right of the pumping station, until you emerge on the tarmac road, a short distance from the Gaulter Gap row of cottages. Keep to the road as it bends round behind the cottages (the coast path continues on at this point, to Kimmeridge beach). Just before the road reaches a gate, by a bridge over a little stream, turn left at a stile, following a field path back towards Kimmeridge village. (A few yards further along the road is a conveniently sited toilet block).

Follow the footpath towards a stone barn (the little stream is to your right). At the barn, cross a stile and take the right-hand path, keeping ahead alongside the stream. Two stiles together will take you into a larger field, beside a second stone barn. Keep ahead across the field (the stream temporarily wanders off to the right, before returning to run once again beside the path). At the far corner of the field, cross a stile and take a path across a little wooden bridge over the stream. The houses of Kimmeridge village are now very near. Follow the path, and enter the left-hand side of a small field. At the end of the field, you emerge by a stile into Kimmeridge's main street.

Walk up the road, past a lovely collection of thatched stone cottages, to the church. As the road bends round to the right, continue straight ahead, walking up a flagged stone path beside the churchyard. Leave the churchyard, and cross the big field, aiming for the gap almost directly ahead. You will quickly emerge at a stile, a few yards from the quarry car park.

13. Lulworth Cove – Flowers Barrow – Tyneham – Worbarrow – Lulworth Cove

A seven mile walk along one of the finest stretches of the Dorset coastline, taking 3½ to 5½ hours. Worbarrow is a magnificent bay, whilst the ruins of Tyneham village, occupied by the Army during the last war and not returned subsequently, are still poignant.

Note: This walk is across the Lulworth Army Ranges, and access is not always possible. Check the information boards (at various places, including Lulworth, Stoborough and Corfe), or telephone the Army on Bindon Abbey (0929) 462721. The footpaths are always open from 9 am on Saturdays to 8 am on Mondays, all day on public holidays and daily throughout August.

Starting point Lulworth Cove. Large car park at Lulworth Cove itself. Buses currently run to and from Dorchester, and summer services are also operated from Poole.

Facilities As befits a popular tourist centre, Lulworth Cove is well stocked with restaurants and cafes, and a pub. Toilets. The Youth Hostel at West Lulworth is conveniently placed for walkers along the coast path.

Tyneham village has now been equipped with toilets; no refreshments.

Problems The Army are anxious to ensure that the public does not wander off the designated paths, and the waymarking is suitably efficient. You won't get lost. But be warned: there are four brisk climbs to be tackled. Take them slowly.

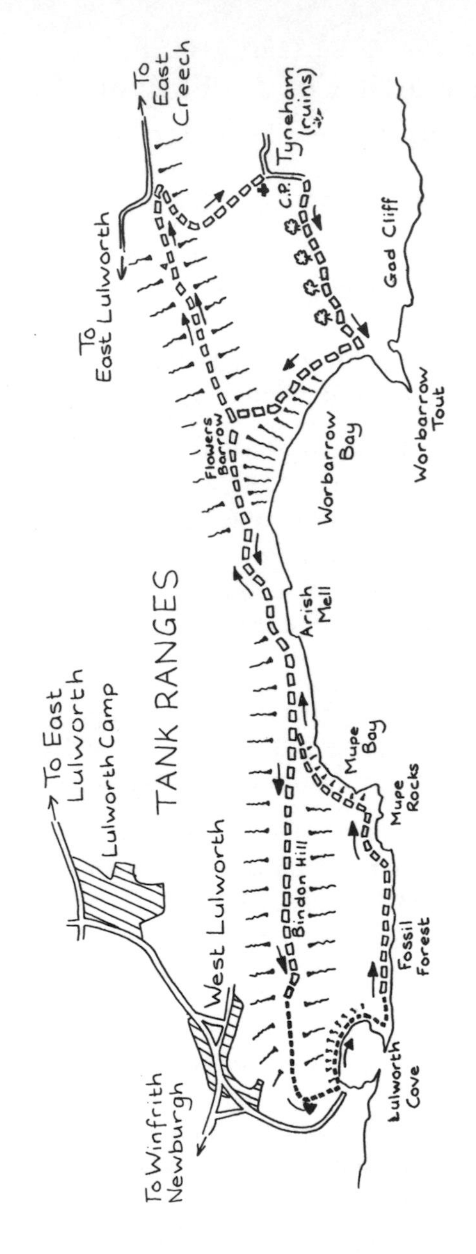

To East Creech
Tyneham (ruins)
C.P.
To East Lulworth
Gad Cliff
Worbarrow Tout
Worbarrow Bay
Flowers Barrow
TANK RANGES
Arish Mell
To East Lulworth Lulworth Camp
Mupe Bay
Mupe Rocks
West Lulworth
Bindon Hill
Fossil Forest
Lulworth Cove
To Winfrith Newburgh

DESCRIPTION

It is in the west that geography lets down Purbeck's claim of being an island. To the south and east, Purbeck is bounded by the English Channel, and anyone entering Purbeck from the north over the River Frome at Wareham does at least have to cross water. But in the west only the tiny heathland stream of Luckford Lake makes any kind of natural boundary – and Luckford Lake itself peters out on the Army ranges somewhere north of Whiteway Hill.

Nevertheless the guide books will tell you that Luckford Lake, and then an invisible line south-west to Arish Mell, the little cove on the coast between Worbarrow and Lulworth, marks the western boundary of Purbeck. The Purbeck Hills themselves finally run into the sea just to the east of Arish Mell.

Since the war, however, the Army firing ranges have provided a much more obvious western boundary to Purbeck than anything nature could provide. Particularly out of the summer tourist season, when the range walks and the hill road from Steeple to Lulworth are closed to the public, the villages of Kimmeridge, Creech and Church Knowle are often effectively isolated from the rest of Dorset beyond.

By either definition, therefore, this walk begins and ends outside of 'proper' Purbeck. Lulworth Cove is well known: a small, almost circular bay, which has been popular with visitors for many years (John Keats visited it in 1820, and a local legend has it that Napoleon himself once landed one dark night, perhaps to reconnoitre a suitable invasion site for his troops). In summer, Lulworth Cove is busy: too many cars and coaches for the narrow Dorset lanes.

When the Ranges Walks are open, however, this walk will enable you to leave the crowds behind. There is spectacular coast scenery to be enjoyed, as well as the particular interests of the Fossil Forest, just inside the Army Ranges, and of the

Iron Age hill-fort at Flowers Barrow. There is also public access, when the Walks are open, to two rocky bays, at Mupe and Worbarrow.

There is no access, however, to the little cove of Arish Mell, once a remote and unspoilt corner of the Dorset Coast, as attractive as its name. T. E. Lawrence – Lawrence of Arabia – who lived the last years of his life in Clouds Hill Cottage on the heath north of Bovington used to swim there with friends. The little beach was, apparently, well-known for its brightly coloured pebbles, which according to one account were collected by local men and women, sorted by hand and then run up the beach in wheelbarrows to be taken away by lorries to end their lives at local pottery works, as decorations on ornamental vases and bowls.

Poor Arish Mell. It is now one of the saddest places in Purbeck. The coast path passes it by, and the beach is out of bounds behind a wire fence and a locked gate. For once, the reason is not the risk of unexploded shells from Army firing practice, but an invisible and more insidious danger. When the atomic research station was build on the heath at Winfrith in the late 'fifties, a pipeline carrying waste from the experimental heavy water reactor was laid to Arish Mell, where the waste is discharged into the sea from an outfall on the beach.

At the time, when the Army had sole access to the area, it must have seemed a perfect solution to what could have been a controversial problem. In recent years, public concern at what may be entering the English Channel at Arish Mell has periodically gained media attention.

Nevertheless, don't let Arish Mell's plight put you off undertaking this walk. For years this area was closed to the public: I suggest you make the most of the limited concession we have now been given to see this beautiful stretch of the coastline for yourself.

DIRECTIONS

The walk begins at Lulworth Cove itself. Turn left on to the beach, and walk about two-thirds of the way along the cove, picking your way over the pebbles. Pass a flight of wooden steps disappearing up from the beach, and almost immediately take a path climbing diagonally up from the cove to a memorial stone on the cliff-top. At this stone turn left, and you will quickly reach the fence which marks the edge of the Army ranges.

Go through the metal gate in the fence (it will be firmly locked if the Range Walks are closed). The path along the cliff edge lies ahead, clearly bounded on both sides by yellow markers.

It is possible to turn right immediately after entering the ranges, and take the steps down the cliff to view the 'Fossil Forest'. The strange lobster-pot shaped fossils are the remains not of trees, but of the algae which built up around the trunks

The Fossil Forest, Lulworth

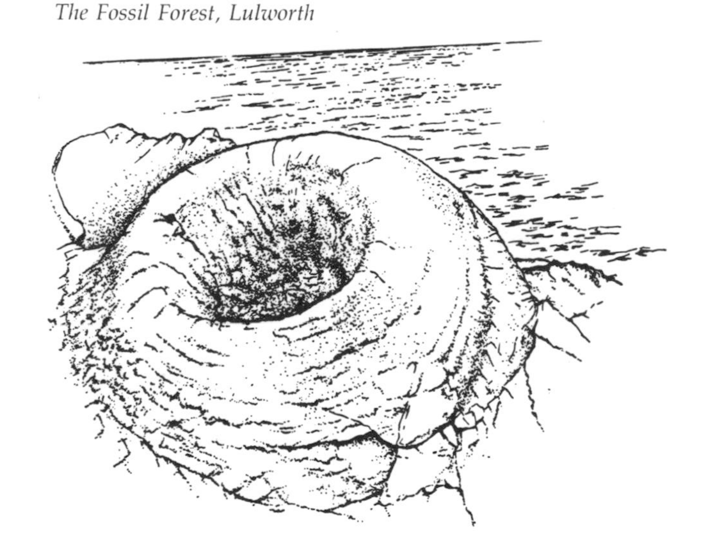

of trees some twenty million years ago. The trees themselves are gone – represented just by the holes in the centre of the fossilised remains.

Even if you choose not to make the diversion, some of the fossilised stumps can be clearly seen from the cliff-path after another few hundred yards, looking like curious cylindrical rocks.

Ahead lies the Purbeck coast: to the right, St Aldhelm's Head closes the view in the distance, while Houns Tout, Swyre Head and the Clavell Tower at Kimmeridge are all visible, and the jagged edge of Gad Cliff also soon comes into sight. The path turns to skirt an inlet, and shortly afterwards some steps lead down to the rocky beach of Mupe Bay.

The path turns along the top of Mupe Bay, and now begins a tough climb up the side of Bindon Hill. At the top, turn right, following the sign to Flowers Barrow. The climb is worth it for the view, which includes the water of Poole Harbour in the distance and the range of Purbeck Hills stretching round towards Swanage.

The path continues gently downhill along a narrow ridge. The cliff edge is directly to the right, while to the left the hill falls sharply to a plain, criss-crossed by the tracks of tanks. Finally the path descends to Arish Mell.

There's another steep climb up from Arish Mell until the first of the ramparts of Flowers Barrow are reached. Although a large part of this Iron Age hill-fort has now fallen into the sea, what is left is still impressive. The path runs parallel to an earth rampart, some thirty yards to the left, until the heart of the fort is reached.

Flowers Barrow occupies a breath-taking position, on the edge of the cliffs, rising to 565 feet above sea-level. It is one of a number of hill forts in this part of Dorset – Maiden Castle near Dorchester being the most famous – which are assumed to have been centres of power for the Durotriges, the Celtic people who lived in this area in the years before the Roman invasion, and who have given modern-day Dorset its name. It seems probable that Flowers Barrow was stormed by Vespasian's Second Legion in the years after AD43.

Flowers Barrow is associated with Purbeck's best-known ghost story, of a Phantom Army which was seen marched from here along the crest of the Purbeck Hills towards Creech in the year 1678. At the time the army seemed only too real to local people: over 100 people are reported to have seen it, and to have heard 'a great clashing of arms'. Among them was the local landowner of Creech Grange, John Lawrence. He and his brother immediately rushed to London to inform the government. Three hundred militia marched to Wareham, and the bridge was barricaded . . . but all for no purpose. The army vanished.

At Flowers Barrow the coastal path turns off to the right; however, our path carries straight ahead, on the ridgeway of what is the final section of the Purbeck Hills. This is a delightful hilltop walk, again with views ahead towards Poole Harbour and the heathland. The path continues past a triangulation stone and then drops down towards the road from Creech to Lulworth. Just before the road is reached, beyond a metal gate, turn sharp right, and cut back down the side of the hill along a dusty track. Tyneham church and the remains of the village are below you. [See introduction to Walk 12 for more about Tyneham].

Pass Tyneham church and the car parking area, through the gate and over a little bridge. Turn right, following the sign to Worbarrow. The track runs down towards the sea, with the tangled undergrowth of Tyneham Gwyle to your right, and the edge of Gad Cliff above you to the left. One fine days, the Isle of Portland is visible, directly ahead. Once at Worbarrow, drop down to the beach, and then cut back up to the right, again making for the yellow way marks.

Worbarrow remains attractive, even though the old fishermen's cottages are now just ruins. New plaques, erected by the County Council's Heritage Coast venture, try to set the scene, but it is hard to image the pre-war bustle that took place when mackerel shoaled in the Bay.

"When a quantity of mackerel were secured in the net the sight was one to be remembered. The fish lay quiet until they had almost reached the shore. Then all at once the water churned and broke in a hundred places simultaneously and fish leapt high into the air, their curved wet bodies glittering with all the colours of the rainbow as they flashed into the sunlight and fell back again into the seething mass below. Women ran knee deep into the waves to help support the weight of mackerel in the straining net and slowly, inch by inch, the heavy catch was dragged out of the sea and up the shelving shore.

"The moment that the shoal was seen to be enclosed a telegram had left the coastguard station and very soon the dealers' carts arrived form Wareham. The fish were counted, packed into boxes and sent off to inland markets still alive and dripping from the sea". (*Tyneham*, Lilian Bond).

The path continues along the edge of Worbarrow Bay, beginning to climb up the side of the chalk downs. This is yet another steep clamber, to take us back once again to Flowers Barrow.

From Flowers Barrow, follow the path back to Arish Mell, and then climb up the hill beyond, until the signpost on the top of Bindon Hill is reached.

Over to the right, the remains of Lulworth Castle can be seen among the trees. From the coast path it appears to be a real fortified mediaeval castle: but appearances are deceptive. It was built in the early seventeenth century as a country house, and the castle fortifications are merely an architectural whim. Sadly, the castle was completely gutted in a fire in 1929; but it is now partly restored and in the hands of English

Heritage.

The Weld family, the local landowners, allowed a group of Trappist monks from France to live nearby during the Napoleonic period, and their presence is still commemorated by the name Monastery Farm on current maps.

At the signpost on Bindon Hill, this time keep straight ahead along the brow of the hill. The track becomes chalky and dusty. Pass the radar station (the hill itself is called Radar Hill), crossing the tarmac approach road, and staying on the brow of the hill. Very shortly, you reach the boundary fence of the Army ranges once again. Ignore the footpaths to the left and right, and keep ahead, walking across the turf, making for a gap in an earthwork boundary.

This last stretch across the turf is a delight. The path drops down, swinging to the left. Cross a well-marked track, and follow a sheep path for a short way. Shortly, over to the right, you will be able to see a small gate into a wood. Strike off to this gate, and then follow the path down through the woods. You'll emerge at a stile directly above Lulworth Cove.

Lulworth Castle

14. Corfe Castle – Scotland Farm – Norden Heath – Blue Pool – Norden Wood – Corfe Castle

A four mile heathland walk, taking 2 – 3½ hours, in an area of Purbeck that's very definitely off the beaten track.

Starting point Corfe Castle. Parking for clients is available behind the Castle View Cafe, on the north side of the castle; or park beside the castle, on the road to Church Knowle. Buses run to Corfe from Swanage and Wareham.

Facilities In Corfe Castle village itself, shops, cafes and pubs. The Castle View cafe is conveniently placed for the beginning and end of the walk. The Blue Pool, a large lake in an old clay-working which has been converted into a beauty spot, has a cafe and tea-room and gift shop (admission charge).

Problems The worst stretch of mud is near New Line Farm, but once past here the ground is firmer. The little link path south of the Blue Pool can be overgrown, as can be stretches of the path to Scotland. In general, considering that this route follows paths which are not walked very frequently, it's relatively easy to find the right way. Almost all the route is waymarked.

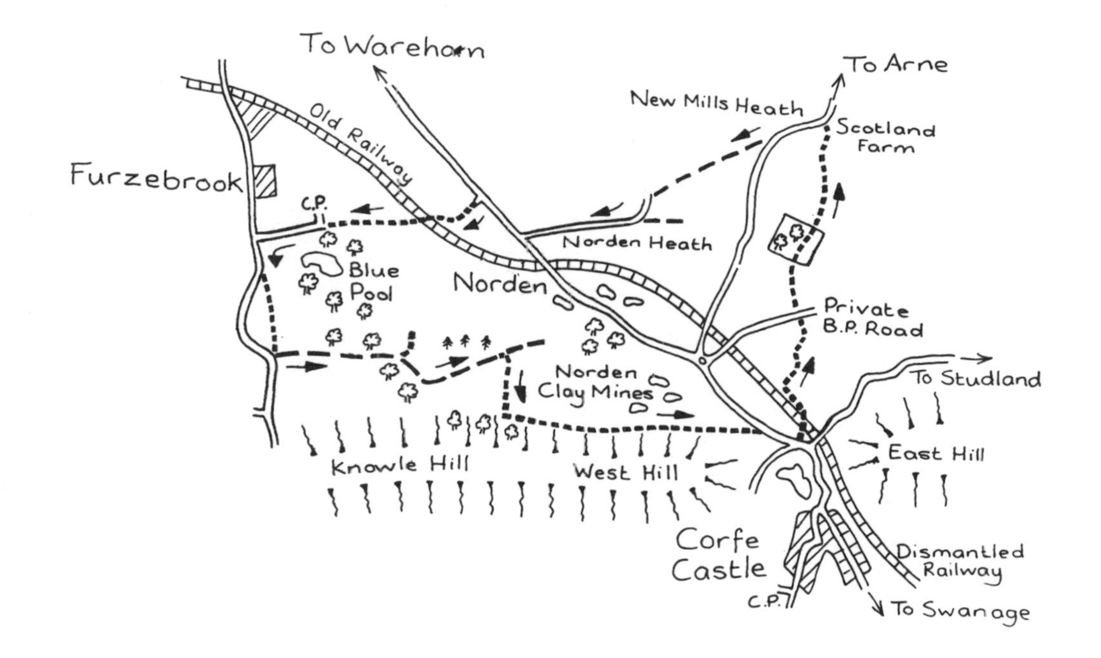

To Wareham
To Arne
New Mills Heath
Scotland Farm
Old Railway
Furzebrook
C.P.
Norden Heath
Blue Pool
Norden
Private B.P. Road
Norden Clay Mines
To Studland
East Hill
Knowle Hill
West Hill
Corfe Castle
Dismantled Railway
C.P.
To Swanage

DESCRIPTION

I might as well be honest: when I first came to select the walks in this book, this particular walk wasn't among them. Why should anyone want to walk north from Corfe Castle on to the heathland, I reasoned, when they could head east or west along the top of the Pubeck Hills, or turn south and make for the coast? But I've changed my mind. After all, the heathland is important to Purbeck not just geographically – over half of the land area is heath – but also economically.

Less well known than the Purbeck marble and stone industry, but equally important in terms of its history, has been the ball clay industry, which – like the marble – has been dug since Roman times. Hundreds of thousands of tons have been excavated over the centuries and taken by sailing boat, railway or lorry to the pottery areas of Staffordshire, or exported throughout the world. From Goathorn in the east to Povington, now in the Army ranges to the west, the heathland bears the scars of this industry.

Clay is still important today: English China Clay have a large works at Furzebrook. Normally this side of Purbeck is hidden from visitors – though many people unknowingly enjoy one of the unplanned end-results of the clay industry when they visit the Blue Pool, formerly one of the largest of the open-cast pits on the heathland.

As well as the Blue Pool, this walk also skirts several other former clay-mining areas, which have now reverted to a semi-natural state.

Norden Wood, which the Nature Conservancy has designated a site of special scientific interest, is particularly attractive. There's also two short stretches, near Scotland Farm and Norden, of real heathland walking – last time I walked near Scotland, a young deer sprang away across the heather from almost under my feet.

Although local authorities have a duty to maintain footpaths, walkers know from bitter experience that a right of way on the map is no guarantee that anything will exist on the ground. Until recently several of the rights of way followed in this walk were very difficult to use: now fortunately things are different. You should find the paths waymarked, and relatively easy to follow.

As elsewhere in Purbeck, a large measure of the thanks for this must go to local walkers, and in particular to members of the Ramblers Association, who have campaigned to ensure that Purbeck's footpaths are saved, and are properly maintained and waymarked. If you enjoy this walk (as I'm sure you will) and have enjoyed the others, consider giving your support to their efforts, by joining the Ramblers Association (members receive a regular magazine, as well as the opportunity to participate in their local and regional groups). The Ramblers Association can be contacted at 1-5 Wandsworth Road, London SW8 2XX (01-582-6878).

DIRECTIONS

Take the path which climbs up from a corner of the old quarry behind the Castle View Cafe. Cross a stile, and almost immediately turn right over another stile, to reach the old railway line. Cross the track-bed into a grassy field, and then turn left, walking alongside the railway embankment.

Leave the field by another stile into some rough woodland. Make sure you take the path which continues to run alongside the railway, and carry on until you arrive nearly alongside an old tumbledown bridge over the railway. At this point turn right.

For a short time, from here on, the path follows the track of another railway: not the B.R. branch line, but the old narrow-gauge railway which used to run from the Norden clay pits to the edge of Poole Harbour. (The bridge over the

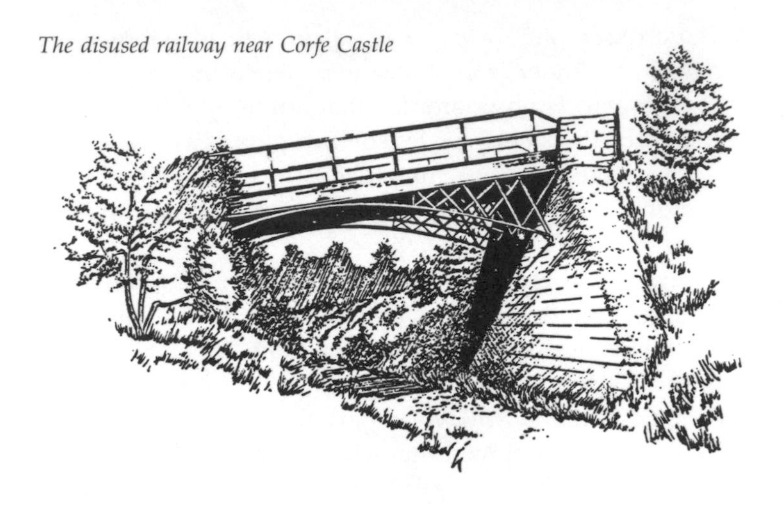
The disused railway near Corfe Castle

railway was itself used by the clay trains.)

A short stretch of railway, with the unusual gauge of 3′ 9″, had been built in in the 1860s from pits near Goathorn to the Harbour, operated by one small locomotive informally nicknamed Tiny. However, in about 1906, this railway was extended from Goathorn across the heath to the pits near Norden, to replace an earlier plateway (a rail road with L-shaped rails and unflanged wagons) which had been constructed at the beginning of the nineteenth century from Norden to Middlebere wharf, and which was now at the end of its useful life. At this state Tiny was joined by a more powerful locomotive, Thames, and together these two engines operated the line until just before the last war. Thereafter, it was decided to send all the clay away by the main Swanage railway, and the line to Goathorn was taken up. A mile or two of track between the clay pits at Norden and the main railway were left, and regauged to the much more common 1′ 11½″. The celebrated engine Russell, now restored and operating the

Welsh Highland Railway in north Wales, operated on this line for a time. The line finally closed in about 1971, and all the clay is now taken from Norden by lorry.

Follow the path, skirting an old clay pit to the right. The path quickly settles down beside a fence. Keep the fence on your left until you emerge at a stile over the new private road to the Wytch Farm oil field, constructed by BP. Cross the road, climb a few steps, and carry on over a stile into a large field. Keep directly ahead, and you will shortly see a stile at the far side of the field. Turn half left into a little wood of silver birch and bracken. The path meanders through the wood, before finally emerging at the edge of a large field.

Walk almost straight across this field and at the far side you will find a substantial stile. The path continues ahead, and then right, through another patch of woodland before heading across the middle of a scrubby meadow, to emerge through gorse and heather into a short stretch of real heathland. Follow the path through some high gorse bushes, until a tarmac road is reached.

Just to the right before the road, the stone-built Scotland Farm can be briefly seen. Scotland has been described as one of the most attractive of the Purbeck stone farms. An inscription above the lintel dates it to 1665, and it has been suggested that the stone used for the building came from the walls of Corfe Castle, destroyed just a few years earlier: this would have been much more convenient than bringing stone all the way from the quarrying areas of Purbeck.

Turn left, and walk along the road a short way. When the road turns abruptly left, carry on ahead, along a well-defined bridle path. There is no danger of getting lost for the next half-mile. The track runs completelly straight between green fields, carved out of the heathland. Finally the track arrives at some farm buildings. Turn left on to a made-up road, and follow this road round a ninety-degree bend. Carry on along this road, past some houses, until the main

Barn at Scotland Farm

Corfe-Wareham road is reached.

Turn right, and walk alongside the main road for a few hundred yards. Then take the first left, a roadway signposted to the Motala cocker spaniel kennels. Almost immediately, the road divides; turn half-right. Beside a new house, turn right again; a little track runs off between two fields, to arrive at an impressive white gate on to the railway track.

Once over the railway, a small sign informs you that the area beyond is a nature reserve, dedicated as a site of special scientific interest. Follow what is a well-defined track (officially designated as footpath 13) across gorse and heather clad heathland. After a few hundred yards, the track begins to run to the right of a new metal fence: this is the boundary of the Blue Pool, and the fence separates the paying visitors from the walkers outside. The track continues, and very shortly the entrance to the Blue Pool, and the car park, is reached.

The Blue Pool is featured in most of the popular guide-books to the Purbeck area, and though the water tends more often to be a shade of green rather than bright blue, it is pleasantly wooded, and can be an attractive place to go for a stroll.

The Blue Pool was originally a clay pit, operated by the firm of Pike Brothers, one of the two great local clay companies. (The other was the business established by Benjamin Fayle, which operated in Norden and on the heath near Goathorn). The Blue Pool was being worked in the first half of the last century; clay was taken to Ridge, on the River Frome near Wareham, and Pike's constructed a dead-straight track across the heath to Ridge, which can still be followed today. From at least the 1860s, this became a proper narrow-gauge railway, and was later extended west to Cotness, Creech and Povington. A series of engines, named in Latin in sequence from Primus to Septimus were employed on the railway; only one survives, Secundus, which can now be visited in the Birmingham Museum of Science and Industry.

Carry on past the car park, walking along the entrance drive to the Blue Pool. When you arrive at a main road, turn left. As the road swings sharply right, you carry straight ahead. A rather overgrown path through a tangled wood leads straight on, skirting a large old open-cast clay pit to the right (this one has not become filled with water). If the path seems indistinct, persevere. You will shortly emerge at a gate, leading once more on to the road.

Just before the road is reached, a bridle way leads off to the left. Take this path; it should be easier to follow, and is well waymarked, with small blue arrows (the number 7 on the arrows refers to the official designation of the path). The path runs on through a pleasant wood, skirting old clay workings both left and right.

You will shortly arrive at a junction of paths; a footpath continues ahead, but keep to the bridlepath, which turns right, and crosses a little stream. In due course, the path emerges at the right-hand edge of the wood, with green fields to your right, and beyond, the range of the Purbeck Hills. Keep along this path, passing yet another small clay pool to the left. Shortly beyond here, turn right, over a stile, to enter a small field. A footpath runs up the right side of the field, then joins a short muddy stretch of farm track, before entering a second field straight ahead.

Cross this field, keeping direcly ahead, making for a stile and gate at the foot of the hills. Once over this stile, turn sharp left, ignoring another better-defined path which climbs half-left up the hill.

The path continues for a considerable distance along the bottom of the hill, through rough ground invaded by bracken and scrub. It's impossible to go wrong – just carry on, keeping the boundary fence to your left, and admiring the occasional views down over the heathland to Poole Harbour. After perhaps half a mile, the waste tips of the clay workings of Norden come alongside, and finally the path emerges at a stile, directly below Corfe Castle. Cross the stile, but continue to walk beside the boundary fence. Ignore a path off to your left; instead, cross another stile into a large grassy field. Cross the field, heading slightly right, and you emerge on the main Corfe-Wareham road, just a few yards from the Castle View cafe at Corfe.

15. Arne – Shipstal Point – Arne

A final gentle 1 – 1½ hour walk across heathland to the peaceful waters of Poole Harbour. This two mile walk makes use of nature trails and footpaths created by the Royal Society for the Protection of Birds, who own an extensive nature reserve in the area.

Starting point Arne village. Arne is a small isolated village on the edge of the heathland; roads lead to it from Norden, near Corfe Castle, and Stoborough near Wareham. Park in the RSPB car park on the edge of the village. No public transport.

Facilities Toilets attached to the car park. A toy and musical box museum has recently been opened in the village.

Problems None! The route taken includes RSPB footpaths which are not rights of way, and which will not be shown on your Ordnance Survey map.

DESCRIPTION

There's nothing at all arduous about this final walk, a little bonus at the end of the book as a reward for previous exertions. The walk leads you across the nature reserve maintained by the Royal Society for the Protection of Birds to one of the most peaceful corners of Poole Harbour.

The RSPB's nature reserve covers over 1200 acres around Arne, and keen nature lovers should contact the RSPB direct, to arrange to join one of the regular parties into the reserve. Public access is much more limited, with one solitary right-of-way from Arne to Shipstal, though this walk makes use of a number of other short paths created by the RSPB. At Arne humans must take second place to wildlife, and especially to the elusive but attractive little Dartford Warbler, one of Britain's rarest birds.

It was mainly because the heathland around Arne provided one of the very few habitats where the Dartford Warbler bred that the RSPB acquired a reserve in this area. The very cold winter of 1962-3 almost entirely wiped out the bird – there were reported to be only two pairs in 1965. Fortunately, numbers have slowy increased since then.

However, the RSPB are all too aware that another hard winter could undo this progress. Over a hundred years ago, in the 1880s, other spells of cold weather almost wiped out the species from Britain, even though at one stage it had been widely distributed throughout southern England. Another worry for the naturalists, ironically, is hot summers, which bring with them the danger of heath fires.

It's a shame, however, that to protect the Dartford Warbler and the other wildlife on the heath, it seems to be necessary to restrict public access to other parts of the Arne peninsula, including the old clay-exporting quays, along the edge of Poole Harbour.

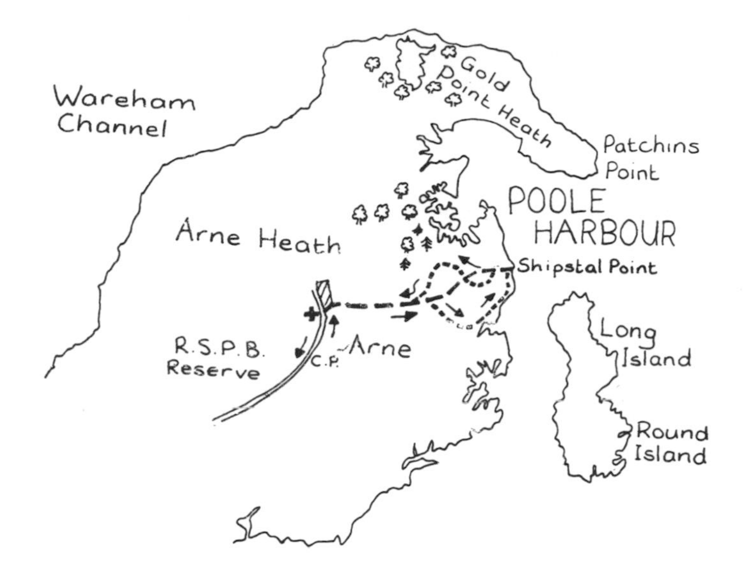

DIRECTIONS

Leave the car park, turn right, and walk along the road towards Arne church and village. The church, like those at Studland and Worth, is dedicated to St Nicholas, and dates from the late twelfth or early thirteenth century. It is a simple building and the main part of the church is still without electricity.

Arne village is really nothing more than the church, a farm and a handful of cottages. Just before you reach the bright new brick-built Arne Farm, turn right down the bridleway signposted to Shipstal. The track runs down between a number of farm fields, before entering woodland.

As you arrive at the woods, turn right along a little footpath. To your right is the fence of the last farm field. Follow the path through a pleasant wood with fine sweet chestnut and oak trees.

The path swings left away from the edge of the wood, and shortly arrives at the salt-flats at the edge of Poole Harbour. These salt-marshes are a familiar sight at the outer reaches of the Harbour, and are dominated by spartina grass, which spreads over nearly 2,000 acres of mud-flats. Follow the duckboards along the harbour edge.

Ahead are two of Poole Harbour's islands, Round Island and Long Island, which spartina grass is busy trying to join into one. The Purbeck side of Poole Harbour is remote, and gives the appearance of being completely undeveloped, though underneath the heathland and harbour waters is the largest on-shore oil field in Europe. When I was a child, Wytch Farm was just a remote heathland farmhouse, which I remember mainly because it appeared to specialise in particularly filthy pigs; now the Wytch Farm oil field is known worldwide. Across the harbour lies Poole, and the contrast between the two sides could not be greater.

Follow the path along the foreshore, until a little sandy beach is reached. The beach finally peters out at a concrete wall. You have arrived at Shipstal Point.

Just before the sea-wall, turn inland, up a sandy track which marks the boundary of the garden of Shipstal Cottage. Immediately past the entrance to the cottage's garden, turn left, and follow a track across the heather to the top of a little hill. At the top, a plaque points out various landmarks. Turn away from the harbour, and drop down the other side of the hill. Cross the path back to the car park, and follow the signs to the RSPB hide.

The path enters woodland, skirting some stagnant, and smelly, pools, where dragonflies can sometimes be seen. At a junction of paths, keep right, again following signs to the hide. Once again, the RSPB have thoughtfully put down duckboards over the wet ground.

The bird hide looks out over the marshes of Arne Bay, and the waters of Wareham channel. As the RSPB makes clear, mud matters: this area of the harbour is a wonderful habitat

Dartford Warbler at Arne

for the waders and wildfowl. Posters on the walls identify some of the more common wading birds which can be seen – and there's space on a noticeboard for you to add anything unusual which you've spotted.

"The redshank is the only breeding species of the saltmarshes, but shelducks nest nearby and their ducklings are a familiar sight on the mudflats", explains the RSPB leaflet about the Arne reserve. "Winter wildfowl are particularly interesting. Red-breasted mergansers, goldeneyes, pintails, shelduck, teal and great crested grebes are frequent visitors and Slavonian grebes are recorded occasionally."

However, it's also worth bird-watching in the woodland areas, where green and great spotted woodpeckers can be seen. Roe deer are frequent visitors, and some Sika, an Asian deer which originally escaped from a herd on Brownsea Island, are also in the area.

From the hide, retrace your steps to a junction of paths, and then turn right, following a path signposted to the car park through the woodland. In due course, the path arrives back at the main bridleway from Arne to Shipstal, at the edge of the farmland. Turn right, and return the way you came to Arne Farm, and your car.